ON TIME, IN FULL
Achieving Perfect Delivery with Lean
Thinking in Purchasing, Supply Chain, and
Production Planning

ON TIME, IN FULL
Achieving Perfect Delivery with Lean Thinking in Purchasing, Supply Chain, and Production Planning

By

Timothy McLean

TXM Lean Solutions Pty. Ltd.

CRC Press
Taylor & Francis Group
Boca Raton London New York

CRC Press is an imprint of the
Taylor & Francis Group, an **informa** business

CRC Press
Taylor & Francis Group
6000 Broken Sound Parkway NW, Suite 300
Boca Raton, FL 33487-2742

© 2017 by Taylor & Francis Group, LLC
CRC Press is an imprint of Taylor & Francis Group, an Informa business

No claim to original U.S. Government works

Printed on acid-free paper

International Standard Book Number-13: 978-1-4987-6864-1 (Paperback)
International Standard Book Number-13: 978-1-138-63218-9 (Hardback)
International Standard eBook Number-13: 978-1-4987-6867-2 (eBook)

Library of Congress Cataloging-in-Publication Data

Names: McLean, Timothy, author.
Title: On time, in full : lean thinking in purchasing, supply chain, and production planning / Timothy McLean.
Description: Boca Raton, FL : CRC Press, 2017.
Identifiers: LCCN 2016045364| ISBN 9781498768641 (pbk. : alk. paper) | ISBN 9781138632189 (hardback : alk. paper) | ISBN 9781498768672 (eBook)
Subjects: LCSH: Lean manufacturing. | Business logistics. | Production planning.
Classification: LCC HD58.9 .M436 2017 | DDC 658.5/03--dc23
LC record available at https://lccn.loc.gov/2016045364

Visit the Taylor & Francis Web site at
http://www.taylorandfrancis.com

and the CRC Press Web site at
http://www.crcpress.com

For Katerina

Contents

Foreword xiii

Acknowledgments xv

Introduction xvii

About This Book xix

Author xxi

1 It Should Be So Simple—Why We Fail to Deliver 1
What You Will Learn in This Chapter 1
So What Is the Problem? 1
Six Reasons Why Companies Have Too Much Stock and Can't Deliver ... 3
    Reason 1: The Customer Cannot Forecast Accurately 3
    Reason 2: Long Lead Times 4
    Reason 3: Big Batch Sizes and Big Shipment Quantities 4
    Reason 4: Material Shortages 6
    Reason 5: Poor Factory Performance 7
    Reason 6: Poor Warehouse and Logistics Practices 8
Summary 8
Key Points in Chapter 1 9

2 Understanding Your Supply Chain 11
What You Will Learn in This Chapter 11
What Is a Supply Chain? 12
The Most Important Supply Chain Metric: Delivery in Full on Time 13
Lead Time: The Key Driver of DIFOT 15
Takt Time: Keeping Track of Whether You Are Keeping up with
Demand 17
Push, Pull, and Flow 17
Understanding Your Supply Chain with a Value Stream Map 19

Summary 25
Key Points in Chapter 2 27

3 Understanding the Future—The Mystery of Forecasting 29
What You Will Learn in This Chapter....................................29
The Promise of Forecasting...29
Can We Tell the Future?...30
Forecasting and the Weather 31
Importance of Significance...32
Building a Forecast 32
Forecasting Raw Material Requirements 34
Low-Volume Products and Materials 36
Generating the Forecast...36
Try Sensitivity Analysis 37
Forecasting Tools 38
Demand Management: Maintaining the Forecast 38
Key Points in Chapter 3..39

4 Can We Do It? Effective Sales and Operations Planning 41
What You Will Learn in This Chapter....................................41
Matching Capacity to Demand: The Foundation for On-Time Delivery 41
Cycle Time and Takt Time: Developing a Simple Rough-Cut
Capacity Model...43
More Advanced Capacity Models 45
Only Analyze Capacity at the Bottleneck Process...................46
Sales and Operations Planning Process 49
Demand Review 51
Supply Review...52
Sales and Operations Planning Meeting 53
Overview of S&OP 55
Key Points in Chapter 4..55

**5 Managing Inventory—If You Do Not Have It, You Cannot
Sell It 57**
What You Will Learn in This Chapter....................................57
Do You Need Inventory?...57
The Other Finished Goods Strategy: Make-to-Order 58
Managing Your Finished Goods Strategy................................59
How Much Inventory Do You Need of Make-to-Stock Items? 60

Calculating Safety Stock...61
Avoiding the Knee-Jerk Response to a Shortage 64
Types of Pull Replenishment..65
Kanban Cards...67
Other Forms of Pull Systems 70
Virtual Kanban...71
Stock-Outs: A Leading Indicator of On-Time, In-Full Performance 71
Inventory Record Accuracy...72
Managing Make-to-Order Supply to Achieve On-Time, In-Full
Delivery 72
Summary 74

**6   What Should We Make Next? The Keys to Production
     Scheduling 77**
What You Will Learn in This Chapter..77
What to Do Next: The Planning Question....................................78
Typical Production Planning Scenario 79
Managing Production Flow with a Pacemaker 81
Finding the Correct Unit of Measure and Pitch Interval 82
Using a Load Leveling Box..82
How Long Should the Pitch Interval Be? 84
Overview of Pacemakers and Pitch 86
Deciding What Product to Make Next at the Pacemaker...............87
Understanding Your Product Mix and Building the Product Cycle 87
Running the Cycle..90
Leveling the Product Mix..91
Product Wheels...91
Summary 92

7   Managing Your Inbound Supply Chain 95
What You Will Learn in This Chapter..95
So Why Do Material Shortages Occur? 97
Deciding the Right Level of Material Inventory............................98
Why Do Shortages Occur?...100
Reducing the Replenishment Interval 100
Reducing Supplier Lead Time...103
Reducing Demand and Supply Variability 106
Summary 107

8   Making Your International Supply Chain Work 109
What You Will Learn in This Chapter..109

Reducing the Lead Time in an International Supply Chain 111
Increasing Shipment Frequency and Reducing Variability 111
Options When Your Monthly Demand Does Not Fill a Container 119
Managing Very Low-Volume Materials 120
Does Importing Still Make Sense? Assessing the Total Cost 121
Summary 123
Case Study: Importing of Custom Sheet Metal Components from
China to Australia 124

9 Working with Suppliers 127
What You Will Learn in This Chapter 127
Are There Any Good Suppliers out There? 127
Understanding Your Supplier 128
Basic Rules for Working with Suppliers 130
Be up Front from the Start 131
Establishing a Service Level Agreement 132
Putting in a Firewall 132
Relationships That Go beyond the Purchase Order 133
Importance of Metrics 134
Managing Poor-Performing Suppliers 136
Summary 138

10 Making the Best Use of Your ERP System 139
What You Will Learn in This Chapter 139
What Is an ERP System? 140
So What Is the Problem with ERP Systems? 141
The Right Time to Purchase an ERP System 145
Selecting an ERP System 145
Successfully Implementing Your ERP 147
Ensure You Have Accurate Master Data 149
Keep Bill of Material Structures and Routings Simple 149
Be Flexible about the Go-Live Date 151
Focus Training and Support after Go-Live 151
Summary 151

11 Managing a Distribution Network 153
What You Will Learn in This Chapter 153
Why Do You Need a Distribution Network? 154
Key Elements of a Distribution Network 154
What Can Go Wrong in a Distribution Network? 155
Designing Your Future State Distribution Network 157

Determine Where You Will Hold Your Finished Goods 159
Minimizing Freight Cost 160
Calculating the Right Level of Inventory 161
Controlling Replenishment 162
Sales and Operations Planning in a Distribution Network 163
Importance of Good Product Management in a Distribution Network ... 164
To 3PL or Not to 3PL? 165
Summary 167

12 Bringing It All Together 169
What You Will Learn in This Chapter 169
Addressing the Six Reasons for Poor On-Time, In-Full Delivery 169
Measuring Supply Chain Performance 171
Improving Your Supply Chain Metrics 172
The Wrong Measures Drive the Wrong Behavior 174
Bringing It All Together: The Industrial Chemicals Case Study 175
Getting Started on Transforming Your Delivery Performance 176
The Right Supply Chain Manager 177
Do You Need a Consultant? 179
A Final Word 179

Index 181

Foreword

Implementing operational excellence or Lean concepts within the "four walls" of your organization is difficult enough. To implement them throughout the supply chain involves another set of challenges. Nevertheless, at some point it must be done. The benefits that a manufacturer or distributor will realize from Lean will be limited by the capabilities of its supply chain. Working in collaborative and creative ways with supply chain partners will maximize the business results for all. Further, it has been said that a customer, current or prospective, is not just buying materials, parts, components, and the like. They are buying the capabilities of an entire supply chain. An organization can incorporate the performance of a strong supply chain in its value proposition when pursuing new customers or defending existing business against the competition. The long-term success of businesses that do just that will be better ensured in the face of ever-demanding customers.

For these reasons, *On Time, In Full* is an important work. Tim McLean provides an easy-to-follow practical approach to building a highly performing supply chain. Early chapters help the reader see through the complexity of a supply chain—the "extended value stream"—and begin to consider how to improve it. The challenges of accurate forecasting, and how to mitigate what has been called the "bullwhip" effect, are covered next. Inventory management and production scheduling practices are then reviewed. The author also addresses the important subject of international supply chains, which can often seem daunting. Together, the chapters represent a step-by-step approach that can be applied to any manufacturing or distribution business.

Don't fall into the trap of believing that you cannot affect significant change in your supply chain. Improvement is always possible. Instead of trying to influence suppliers through negotiations, consider working collaboratively with them in creative ways. The path to a "Lean supply chain" will be different for different organizations. Let *On Time, In Full* be your guide. Begin analyzing your extended value stream and engaging key players, and see where the path leads. It could be the beginning of a great journey.

Drew Locher

Director, Change Management Associates, New Jersey, USA

Acknowledgments

A lot of people helped me with the writing of this book. First, I would like to thank my family for their patience as I spent long hours on weekends completing the manuscript. In particular, I would like to thank my wife, Katerina, for her encouragement and her assistance in proofreading and editing the manuscript. I would also like to thank my publisher, Productivity Press, and their executive editor, Michael Sinocchi, for supporting me with this book and my first book, *Grow Your Factory, Grow Your Profits*.

Many of the case studies through this book are the work of my colleagues at TXM, and I would especially like to acknowledge my business partner, Anthony Clyne; our China consulting director, Justin Tao; and senior consultant Greg Boek. It is their excellent work that is reflected in the case studies in this book. I also particularly appreciate Anthony, Justin, Greg, and my other business partner, Ron Spiteri, for their advice and feedback about the many complex technical aspects of supply chain. It is always good to be able to road test the concepts with experienced experts before letting them loose on the general public in the form of a book. Anthony and Justin also provided many of the photographs used throughout the book.

Equally important are the customers who have supported us along the way and taken the leap of faith to accept our advice. I especially would like to acknowledge Phil and Leon Joyce at Larnec Doors in Swan Hill, Victoria, who have generously allowed their case study to be used in both of my books. As well, Peter Keech at Tasman Chemicals and Jane Chen and Ronny Zhou at Funwick Manufacturing in Kunshan, China, are greatly appreciated for their support.

Drew Locher generously provided a foreword and encouragement. It is an honor to have the author of four excellent books on Lean office processes and Lean product development and the winner of two Shingo awards contribute to this book. I also appreciate the support and ideas of another

Shingo prize-winning author, Ian Glenday, whose work in repetitive flexible supply I reference in Chapters 6 and 8.

Finally, I would like to acknowledge all the supply chain experts who have gone before me and generously contributed their knowledge through their excellent books, some of which I have shared here. There is a lot to learn about supply chain. Hopefully, this book will just be the start and you will follow up the various references that I have provided in order to build up your expertise.

Introduction

The most fundamental requirement for a manufacturing or distribution business is to deliver to customers what they want, in the quantity they want, when and where they want it. It doesn't matter how good your product is, how much the customer likes your salesperson, or how slick your marketing campaign is. If your customers can't get what they want when they want it, they will get it elsewhere and your business is in serious trouble.

I spend most of my days out in factories and warehouses and find that the simple problem of delivering on time, in full every day remains a major challenge for a huge proportion of businesses. This even happens in many cases where the company has the most advanced enterprise resource planning* software. The costs to business and the economy are mind boggling, with billions spent on expediting, overtime, breaking production schedules, scrapping excess stock, last-minute replenishment, empty shelves, and lost sales.

It would seem straightforward enough. You take an order, you pick the goods, and you ship them to the customer. For very small businesses, it is often as simple as that. However, for most businesses the reality is that they handle dozens or even hundreds of orders per day and hundreds or even thousands of transactions and material movements every day to meet those orders.

Why Most Experts Don't "Get It"

The difficulty for manufacturers and distributors is that most experts are focused on the solution rather than the problem. The area of supply chain management theory has become highly contested, with adherents to the different solutions believing theirs to be the "one true way" to the exclusion

---

* Enterprise Resource Planning (ERP) software are systems designed to manage and automate the core business processes involved in delivering products to a customer.

of all others. Whether the proposed solution is the traditional supply chain management approach, with heavy reliance on forecasts, software, and complex business rules; the Lean approach; or the theory of constraints, most of the books I read will promote this one solution to the exclusion of all others. For example, many Lean purists will argue that you should *never* use a forecast for replenishment and instead use only Kanban or just-in-time supply. This is a great system, but what if your supplier is on the other side of the world and your lead time is measured in months? On the other hand, the supply chain management gurus mock "low-tech" solutions like Kanban cards and insist building to a forecast is the only sensible and modern way to manage a supply chain. No wonder so many operations and planning professionals are confused.

My personal view is a little different. Every supply chain is unique, and while many of the symptoms of poor delivery are common (such as excessive inventory combined with frequent stock shortages), the root causes and the solution will vary from business to business. The aim of this book is to help you understand what is going wrong and select the best approach to solve the problems in your business. That solution may involve a combination of enterprise resource planning, Lean, and practical business common sense. It may borrow from the American Production Inventory Control Society* playbook or the Lean approach, it really doesn't matter. What matters is that it enables your business to deliver the right products to your customers at the right time and in the right quantity.

---

* The American Production Inventory Control Society is one of the peak bodies for supply chain management thinking.

About This Book

This book is designed as a practical guide to solving your problems in your supply chain and thereby delivering to your customers what they want and when they want it. The chapters are arranged in a logical sequence that will hopefully enable you to understand your supply chain problem, diagnose the root cause, and develop an end-to-end solution. I have also, however, tried to make each chapter stand alone, so if you don't have time to read the whole book, you can select chapters you feel are relevant to you (e.g., forecasting or enterprise resource planning systems) and just choose to focus on those. It is also a short book covering a large subject. Therefore, I have tried to include references to books that I have read and recommend so you can do more detailed study on particular topics.

Author

Tim McLean has a 30-year career in applying Lean in manufacturing and supply chain across a range of industries. This is McLean's second book, with his first book being *Grow Your Factory, Grow Your Profits: Lean for Small and Medium-Sized Manufacturing Enterprises*, released by Productivity Press in December 2014.

McLean was first introduced to Lean and operational excellence in the late 1980s as a young production manager of a small plastics extrusion plant, part of German global chemical manufacturer Hoechst AG. McLean went on to hold a range of manufacturing and supply chain management roles across the plastics molding, packaging, printing, and chemicals industries for major companies, including Hoechst AG, Amcor, and PPG. McLean was fortunate to be coached by a succession of mentors steeped in the principles of Lean. As an operations manager and general manager, he then faced the real challenge of applying these theories to drive performance in his plants.

After a successful 16-year career leading manufacturing and supply chains, McLean set up TXM, a consulting business in Australia aimed at helping other manufacturing leaders like himself to achieve their goals. TXM has since grown to be a leading specialist Lean consultancy, operating from offices in Australia, the United States, the United Kingdom, and China, and carrying out a diverse range of projects, primarily in manufacturing, distribution, and agribusiness. In line with McLean's experience and values, TXM has developed a reputation for delivering practical outcomes for the diverse range of businesses he has worked with.

Through his corporate and consulting career, McLean faced a wide range of complex supply chain challenges, including implementation of enterprise resource planning systems, international outsourcing, distribution network redesign, and plant and warehouse consolidation. It is much of this practical experience that he has drawn upon in this book.

McLean and TXM have an extensive network around the Asia Pacific region, and he is a frequent speaker at industry events, including the Association for Manufacturing Excellence Conferences, Lean Enterprise China, the International Society of Pharmaceutical Engineers, and Australian Manufacturing Week. McLean publishes regular blogs on a range of Lean, manufacturing, and supply chain topics at www.txm.com and also regularly contributes articles to trade publications, including *Australian Manufacturing Technology*, *Manufacturers Monthly*, *Australia-China Connections*, and *China Sourcer Magazine*.

Chapter 1

It Should Be So Simple—Why We Fail to Deliver

What You Will Learn in This Chapter

- *How to recognize whether your supply chain is not functioning correctly*
- *The key root causes of poor delivery performance*
- *Why your enterprise resource planning system may be making the problem worse rather than better*
- *How to understand your supply chain using a value stream map*

So What Is the Problem?

Around the time I sat down to write the first chapter of this book, I was invited to the annual sales conference of a new customer. The customer was a company that manufactured and distributed a large range of industrial chemicals, mainly for use in the dairy industry and commercial cleaning. Their products were sold through farm retail chains and cleaning chemical distributors and often sat on the shelf next to very similar competitive products.

The reason the CEO invited me to the sales conference was to provide some reassurance to the sales team that their new Lean project was going to focus on addressing the business's chronic delivery problems. After an initial introduction to the project and my background and credentials, what followed was a fairly heartbreaking hour listening to the frustration of the sales representatives from all around Australia. Their concerns represented a litany of pretty much everything that goes wrong in supply chains. Some of their comments were

■ *Why do we run out of stock of our most important products when we have so many slow-moving products on the shelf?*
■ *Why is the stock never accurate on our computer system?*
■ *What should I say to a customer when he asks me when an item on back order will be delivered? Nobody at the factory seems to know.*
■ *Why is the production manager the only one who seems to know when things will get made? Most of the time I can't contact him, and I don't feel I should need to contact him anyway.*

The salespeople at this business estimated that they spent at least two hours per day parked by the side of the road on their phones trying to find out when a product would be available. They lacked confidence to win new business because they did not believe that the goods that they promised to the customer would be delivered on time. The products were really good, customers wanted them, but if they could not get reliable supply, customers bought a competitive product—even if the quality was not as good as theirs.

Like many businesses in this situation, relationships between sales and production were toxic. The production manager resented the constant badgering calls demanding product almost as much as the sales team resented having to make those calls.

However, the frustrations of the sales team were just the tip of the iceberg. Toward the end of the discussion, the chief financial officer (CFO), who was also at the conference, pointed out quietly that despite all the frustration about shortages and backorders, the business had more than three months' worth of inventory. When this was added to the two months it typically took for customers to pay their bills, the company had to wait an average of five months from the time it purchased packaging and materials to the time customers paid their bills. This placed an enormous cash flow burden on the business and meant it was saddled with debt to fund all that excess working capital.

So to sum up, missed deliveries, shortages, disappointed sales teams, and frustrated customers go hand in hand with excess inventory, obsolete write-offs, and cash flow difficulties. It sounds like a paradox: too much stock, but constant shortages impacting on delivery. How can this occur?

Six Reasons Why Companies Have Too Much Stock and Can't Deliver

In my experience, there are a number of reasons for the situation that faced our client described above. You are likely to recognize some or all these in your business.

Reason 1: The Customer Cannot Forecast Accurately

This is not actually a reason for poor performance; it is an excuse. The oldest saying in business is that "the customer is always right." To me, this saying should not be taken literally. What it really means is that the customer can decide who they purchase from. Therefore, if you cannot meet the customer's unreasonable unforecasted needs, they will purchase what they need from someone else, if at all possible. This begs the question of whether your company is truly able to serve this customer, and whether in fact you might better allow this customer to buy from someone else. However, if the customer is one you want to keep and you are unable to meet their "unreasonable" needs, then consider that problem as yours, not theirs.

So why am I saying all this in the context of forecasting? The reason is that if the customer is unable to provide you an adequate forecast and you want to keep that customer, then you had better find another way to meet their needs that does not rely on the forecast.

There may be very good reasons why the customer cannot provide a forecast. Perhaps they simply cannot anticipate and forecast future demand. If you consider the supply of ice cream, for example, demand is totally dependent on the weather. Perhaps factors beyond their control impact demand. Builders, for example, are often a source of complaints from my customers in the construction materials industry. However, the life of a builder can be very unpredictable, work can be delayed by other tradespeople held up working on other sites, other materials (other than yours) may be delivered late, unexpected issues on the job site can delay progress, or bad weather can stop work all together.

We can also compound the forecasting problem internally. Flagging sales can generate a last-minute promotion, which strips the shelves of stock to meet normal demand. Poor planning around product development can lead to large imbalances in supply and demand for new products and obsolete stock of old products. Overly generous promises can be made to customers without consideration of the business's ability to deliver.

Fortunately, the problems we generate internally are *slightly* easier to manage than problems created by our customers or market conditions. Chapter 4 will introduce sales and operations planning, an effective way to ensure that the various functions in the business talk to each other regularly about demand and the ability of the business to supply that demand. Before that, we are going to have a hard look at the pros and cons of forecasting in Chapter 3.

Reason 2: Long Lead Times

When we complete a value stream map* of a process or supply chain, we calculate the lead time in the process. I usually describe this as the time it takes for one unit of raw material to travel from the receiving dock through the plant to shipping. In an extended supply chain, you can take this further and consider the lead time to be from when your supplier receives an order for material and then travels through their process, through your factory or warehouse, through your distribution network, and finally to the customer. This can be a long time, and the longer it is, the worse your supply chain challenge can be. When you add up all these individual lead times for scheduling the production, sourcing the materials, manufacturing the goods, and packing and shipping the goods, total lead times of six months or more are not unusual. This means that the materials you order today will not be delivered to the customer as finished goods for six months. As a result, you need to know or make a judgment call on what specific products and quantities the customer will need in six months' time. This is very difficult, if not impossible. The difference between your six-month-old estimate and what the customer actually needs can be very large. If you get it wrong, then you most likely will have to expedite the materials that you now need and will be faced at the same time with excess stock of products that you have no immediate use for.

Lead time is an evil at every step of the supply chain, and one of the most powerful aspects of the Lean approach is a relentless focus on reducing lead time through reducing non-value-added time. In Chapter 2, we will discuss value stream mapping to reduce lead time in your operations and supply chain.

Reason 3: Big Batch Sizes and Big Shipment Quantities

It is easy to rationalize why big batches or large shipments are "efficient." Fewer setups, less downtime, and more stable processes mean that big

---

* A value stream map is a special type of process map used in Lean Thinking. It maps the flow of a product along with the information that controls that flow. It is used to highlight and eliminate waste in the flow.

batches appear to lead to greater efficiency. Large shipments mean you can ship "full containers" and save money on freight. You may get discounts from suppliers from ordering large shipments. In manufacturing, your measures of efficiency, such as "overall equipment effectiveness," will go up when you increase batch sizes. The problem is that big batch sizes and large shipments compound your supply chain problem. The first reason is that they extend your lead times. This is because big batch sizes take longer to run, and it takes longer to consume the inventory from large shipments. Let's say you make 30 different products and aim to run one batch per day. As a result, on average you will only make an individual product once every 30 days. If an order comes in, then the customer may need to wait up to 30 days (on average 15 days) while you complete batches of other products before they get their orders fulfilled. This additional lead time adds no value, but increases supply chain risk and the amount of inventory your customer needs to hold. Likewise, big shipment quantities take a long time to consume, which means that you only replenish infrequently. The greater the gap between one delivery and the next, the greater the chance that demand will unexpectedly increase, leading to a shortage before the next delivery arrives.

Big batches and large shipment sizes also compound what is called the "bullwhip effect" (also known as the Forrester effect). This effect, which I discuss more in Chapter 10, is the phenomenon whereby the variation in demand for a product is amplified as you go up the supply chain. This is because the production batch or minimum order size might be many times greater than the typical customer purchase quantity. As a result, customer purchases will not trigger upstream demand until a whole batch or order quantity has been consumed. This process is repeated at each step up the supply chain and this artificial demand pattern (caused by batching) is built into forecasts, multiplying demand variation. Therefore, we often see products with very stable consumer demand through the year (e.g., laundry powder or toilet paper) where the demand on suppliers two or three steps up the supply chain (e.g., packaging suppliers) varies wildly from week to week and month to month.

Of course, if the batch size was equal to the customer order size, then an order for 10 units would trigger a batch for 10 units. Demand would not be amplified. Increasing batch sizes or order quantities, which is often aimed at stabilizing production (by allowing "longer runs"), will often *increase* volatility in the supply chain, making shortages worse and of longer duration, while at the same time increasing inventory (because bigger batches and less frequent replenishment mean more inventory on average).

Reason 4: Material Shortages

Material shortages are a huge cause of production delays and late deliveries, particularly for complex products with many components, such as machine tools or heavy vehicles. You will note that I have not written "poor supplier performance" as the issue here, although the majority of companies I talk to would blame suppliers for raw material shortages. When I have examined raw material problems in detail, I have found that the majority of material shortages find their root cause in the business itself, not the suppliers.

One major manufacturer of a complex high-technology product suffered more than 100 material shortages per day. This was the number one cause of production delays and late deliveries. When I analyzed the thousands of shortages that had occurred over a year, I found that less than 10% had been caused by the supplier failing to deliver on time and in full. The causes of the remaining 90% lay within my customer's business processes and the operation of their enterprise resource planning (ERP) system.

The reasons for material shortages are many and varied but include poor inventory accuracy, incorrect target inventory levels, infrequent and unstructured ordering (compounding lead times), ordering too much at once, failure to adjust for changing usage patterns, and incorrect and unrealistic lead time assumptions.

For example, the high-technology product manufacturer described above was complaining about the poor service from a supplier of wiring harnesses. That supplier was always late delivering a particular harness assembly that resulted in stock-outs almost every time the product was ordered. When we studied the situation, we found that the supplier was required to meet a standard lead time of eight days for all the products they supplied. However, the problem harness included a cable, a connector, and a small electric motor. The motor was imported from Germany, from a sole supplier that had been specified by our customer, who had a lead time of several weeks, and the harness supplier had been told not to hold stock of motors. Therefore, it was impossible to meet the eight-day lead time requirement and inevitable that the part would stock out every time it was ordered. In this case, inventory of the harnesses was increased and lead time in the customer's ERP system adjusted to reflect reality.

In Chapters 7 through 9, we will discuss how you can design an inbound supply chain that prevents shortages and work with your suppliers to improve supply chain performance.

Reason 5: Poor Factory Performance

As a manufacturing and supply chain manager of 16 years standing and having talked with dozens of factory managers, one could be forgiven in many businesses for believing that poor factory performance is the *only* reason for poor delivery performance. Unfortunately, when goods are not available, the factory manager tends to cop a lot of the blame, even if the root causes of the problem have little to do with his or her team.

Nevertheless, some things are the factory manager's responsibility: frequent machinery breakdowns, labor shortages, and industrial disputes, meeting delivery dates is problematic. However, these problems are usually compounded by material shortages and constant schedule changes (due to demand volatility).

Essentially, we get into a vicious cycle. It works like this. On Monday, we start out with a new production plan and start making Job 1. Unfortunately, the press we are using that was running perfectly happily on Friday now does not want to operate. Therefore, we call maintenance to fix it, who tells us they need to order a part and the press will be out of production for a day.

We now have five operators standing around with nothing to do, so we quickly set up Job 2 from the production schedule on another press. All is well for about an hour, and then an operator comes into the office and says, "Boss, we have run out of part 1234." Part 1234 was scheduled for delivery tomorrow to coincide with the production of Job 2, but now you are doing Job 2 today. You ring purchasing and tell them the problem, and they inform you that they will order a courier and the missing parts will be on site after lunch. However, lunch is still three hours away, so you get the team to set up Job 3 on the schedule. This job has two component parts, a left and a right, but you have used up the stock of part 5678 that's needed for the right-hand part in your unscheduled production of Job 2. Nevertheless, you get the team started on producing left-hand parts and give the purchasing team another urgent order to supply. After lunch, the missing parts 1234 arrive and the second job is completed, and then at 4:30 p.m., the extra stock of part 5678 arrives. The customer has rang informing us that the order for Job 3 is now urgent. You talk to the team and ask who wants to work overtime to finish the right-hand parts. There's a big football game tonight and there are only two takers, so you set up the reduced crew and plan to deliver half the order to the customer tomorrow morning to get them out of trouble.

After one day, the schedule has been changed three times: One order (Job 1) is late, and a second (Job 3) will be short delivered. A third order (Job 2) has been completed, but this was not due until Wednesday anyway, and it has been finished on Monday afternoon—but at least you have it in stock! Does this sound at all familiar? We call it "roadrunner" production because production is stop–start, a bit like the Roadrunner on the *Looney Tunes* cartoon. Roadrunner production causes more and more problems that feed on one another the longer it continues. More and more batches get delayed and rescheduled, more unscheduled batches are run, labor and materials get consumed producing the jobs that *can* run rather than the jobs that *need* to run, and managers spend their whole day expediting to meet the next late or urgent order rather than focusing on solving the problems that will permanently improve performance.

Reason 6: Poor Warehouse and Logistics Practices

Once the goods get out of the factory, poor practices in the warehouse can further contribute to poor delivery outcomes. Inaccurate stock recording can mean that orders are taken and promises made to customers only for the stock to be missing when the operator goes to pick the order. Even if the stock is in the location, incorrect decision-making about inventory levels means that inventory is insufficient to meet customer demand. This problem is compounded by excessively long lead times to replenish stock or long replenishment cycles (the time from one delivery of a particular material to the next).

Poor management of warehouse workload can mean that orders do not get picked and shipped within the agreed time window. Inadequate processes for picking and poor warehouse layout can also contribute to errors where the wrong items or wrong quantities are picked and shipped. Poor communication with freight providers or poor performance by your freight provider can mean goods don't get delivered when they are required, or they don't even get picked up in time from your loading dock. In a distribution network, poor decision-making about where to locate inventory in the network and poor processes for replenishing stock in branch stores can lead to stock being in the wrong place when it is needed."

Summary

The six reasons that I have outlined above explain much of the chaos I see in supply chains. In turn, this chaos is the reason for failure to deliver to customers on time, in full. When you are in the midst of this chaos, it is hard to imagine working your way out of it. However, the pathway to a solution for your business is relatively straightforward and well proven. This book aims to take you through the steps required to address these reasons and build a stable and effective supply chain that delivers on time, in full for your customers every day.

Key Points in Chapter 1

The typical characteristics of a poor-performing supply chain are frequent inventory shortages and poor on-time, in-full delivery combined with high levels of inventory and obsolescence. This occurs for six key reasons:

1. The customer is unable to provide an accurate forecast because they do not know what will happen in the future.
2. Long lead times mean that supply chain decisions have to be made many months in advance.
3. Big batch sizes and large shipment quantities compound long lead times and amplify demand variation through the bullwhip effect.
4. Raw material shortages, usually caused by poor supply chain design rather than the supplier, mean that production is delayed.
5. Instability caused by poor factory performance, shortages, breakdowns, people problems, and so forth, leads to more instability, as the production plan changes frequently.
6. Poor warehouse and logistics practices, such as inaccurate inventory, inadequate inventory levels, poor picking organization and productivity, and poor picking accuracy, further delay and disrupt supply.

Chapter 2

Understanding Your Supply Chain

What You Will Learn in This Chapter

This chapter introduces key supply chain concepts, including

- *The definition of a supply chain*
- *The importance of lead time and the different types of lead time*
- *Takt time as a yardstick for process performance*
- *The difference between push, pull, and flow in a supply chain*
- *Using a value stream map to understand your supply chain*

Not only will you learn the meaning of these concepts, but also you will learn how they impact your business's ability to deliver on time and in full to your customers.

In Chapter 1, we discussed the fact that a range of factors—many outside your organization—can affect your ability to deliver your product to customers on time and in full. Therefore, to improve performance, you need to understand at least some of those external factors, as well as all the factors within your organization. This means gaining a detailed understanding of your supply chain and how it works.

What Is a Supply Chain?

Supply chain is one of those business terms used so frequently and so loosely that its real meaning is often lost. For example, I have met people whose title is "supply chain manager" but whose role may involve any combination of the following activities: planning, purchasing, manufacturing, procurement, freight, or warehousing. The reality is that the term *supply chain* encompasses all those things. In its broadest sense, a supply chain can include all the people, processes, and organizations involved in fulfilling customer demand for a product—from sourcing its raw materials to its delivery to the end user. Just one strand within an automotive supply chain, for instance, may look like Figure 2.1.

When you consider that front fenders are but one element in the manufacture of a car, the total supply chain for this product can be immensely complex. Fortunately, in most cases, you do not need to consider the entire supply chain in order to make improvements. Your ability to influence supply chain participants who are more than one or two steps either upstream or downstream from your organization is limited. However, it is worthwhile remembering that the operation of your supply chain, and the constraints it operates within, may be dictated by factors several steps removed from your

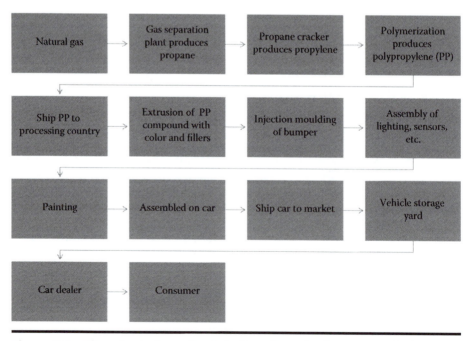

Figure 2.1   Flowchart of supply chain for a front fender on a typical car.

organization. Over them, you have no control, but you will still need to plan for and mitigate their influence on your supply chain.

The best way to describe the supply chain is that it is the series of steps and processes by which value is added to a product, and through which it is delivered to an end customer. This naturally leads to an effective tool for understanding the supply chain—the value stream map, which we will discuss later in the chapter.

The Most Important Supply Chain Metric: Delivery in Full on Time

Delivery in full, on time (DIFOT) is the ultimate measure of the performance of your supply chain. The *purpose* of your supply chain is to deliver to your customer the products they need in the quantity they need, when they need them. DIFOT directly measures how well your supply chain is fulfilling this core purpose. It would be inconceivable for a business not to measure profit or cash flow. It should be equally inconceivable for a manufacturing or distribution business not to manage DIFOT. Unfortunately, many businesses, including the overwhelming majority of small and medium-sized businesses, do not measure DIFOT at all.

DIFOT in its simplest form is simply the ratio of the number of orders that were delivered on time, with all the ordered items supplied in the quantity required on the day that the customer required them, to the total number of orders shipped.

$$\text{DIFOT} = \frac{(\text{Number of orders delivered on time and in full})}{(\text{Total number of orders shipped})} \times \frac{100\%}{1}$$

In a small business, it can be as simple as counting up the orders at the end of the day, and recording the number shipped on time and in full compared with the total orders shipped. If you have an enterprise resource planning (ERP) system, then DIFOT is often a standard report that can be generated in the system. Ideally, DIFOT should be recorded every day, which most systems allow.

There is often a lot of debate about how DIFOT is measured. In particular, companies often have complex rules about due dates. For example, your customer may place an order with a lead time that is shorter than the lead time you can achieve and that has been agreed with the customer. In this case, you may decide to agree at the time of order with the customer to deliver at a later date. This is called "first agreed date." Purists would say that this is already DIFOT failure. I am less concerned about this and do not have a particular problem with companies measuring DIFOT based on first agreed date. However, I would consider that agreeing a further change to the due date is a DIFOT "miss."

A simpler way to measure DIFOT is just to measure it against your standard delivery lead time. For example, if your standard is that orders placed before a cutoff time are shipped on the same day, then you simply measure DIFOT against your achievement of that standard.

It is also likely that you will find it very difficult to measure *delivered* in full and on time, because you may not know exactly when the customer receives your goods. This can be further complicated by delays in the customer receiving your goods once they are on site. Therefore, most businesses actually measure *shipped* on time and in full. If your customer is local and your shipping company reliable, then attempting to record when the goods actually arrived at the customer is not necessary. The exception is long supply chains, such as export markets. In this case, the variable lead time of the international supply chain may be a major factor in whether products are delivered on time. Often, it will be your overseas branch that captures DIFOT. Otherwise, you will need to rely on information provided by your shippers.

Whichever way you measure DIFOT, the most important thing is that your measurement reflects your actual performance in the eyes of the customer. In many cases, particularly when your customer is a large business, they will measure your DIFOT performance themselves. It is critical you measure DIFOT in the same way as your customer. If you consider your customer measure unfair or inaccurate, then you need to have a discussion to reconcile your measures. There is no point measuring DIFOT at 98% when your customer measures your performance to be 85%. You may be patting yourself on the back, while your customer is rating you as a bad supplier.

Even if your customer does not measure your DIFOT, it is important that you align their perception of your service. This might involve you sharing your DIFOT performance with them when you have regular customer meetings. If the feedback in these meetings is that you are not a reliable supplier, it is important to listen and understand the reasons for this perception. Look for particular examples and make sure that you do bridge gaps in their perception of your performance. Often, these discussions will reveal significant opportunities to improve your supply chain performance. Delivering improved performance based on customer feedback will develop great customer relationships. On the other hand, using DIFOT statistics to argue your customer is getting great service when their perception is that your service is poor will have the opposite effect on your relationships.

Lead Time: The Key Driver of DIFOT

Time is the most critical dimension in your supply chain. The key to delivering products on time and in full is developing a process and a supply chain that can respond to customer demand as fast as or faster than the customer requires or expects. Lead time is the key measure of time, and there are a number of different lead times that you need to consider.

The most important lead time is your expected customer order lead time. This is the length of time the customer is prepared to wait—from placing their order to receiving their goods. This can vary enormously, depending on the type of product, the way it is distributed, the customer's location, market expectations (i.e., what the competitors do), and the degree to which a product is customized to meet a customer's individual needs.

So, what is an acceptable lead time for customer orders? What the competition offers is not the only factor. In markets where competition is low, competing suppliers may impose a longer lead time on their customers' orders. This can be a very cozy arrangement for suppliers, but it does carry an element of risk. Often, longer lead times make it hard for customers to plan their operations, and respond to the demands of their own customers. In that case, customers dissatisfied with the lead time in their market will look for suppliers who can better the existing players' time. They may also be eager to facilitate the entrance of a new competitor. As a result, the most important determinant of the acceptable customer order lead time is, unsurprisingly, what the customer needs.

To determine whether your business can meet the required customer order lead time consistently, you need to calculate your order fulfillment lead time.

Order fulfillment lead time is the time from customer order receipt to customer order delivery. As a result, it is the sum of the lead times associated with two flows within your process:

■ The information processing lead time, which extends from the time the customer order arrives via phone, fax, or e-mail until the order is released to production at the pacemaker process or released to the warehouse for picking

■ The part of the processing lead time from the pacemaker, through all the subsequent processing, picking, and distribution steps, until the completed order is received by the customer

If your order fulfillment lead time exceeds the delivery lead time that you have promised your customer, then you have immediately found a key reason for late deliveries. It may seem surprising, but we have found lead times of up to 12 days for customers who were promised an order lead time of less than 4 days. In this case, the supplier spends time furiously expediting "urgent" orders, and negotiating later delivery dates for other orders. The fact that the long order fulfillment lead time simply makes it impossible to consistently deliver on time is often hidden, until it is revealed by the value stream map.

Another key lead time in your process is the replenishment lead time. This is the lead time from placing an order with suppliers until you receive that order. A variant of this lead time occurs when the replenishment of work-in-progress materials is triggered. If you did not have any inventory in your process, then the order fulfillment lead time would equal your order processing time, plus your internal processing time, plus your longest replenishment lead time. In other words, when you received the order, you would order raw materials, wait for them to be delivered, and process them from start to finish, before your customer receives the product. This can lead to extremely long lead times, and usually, customers will not tolerate waiting this long for their products (in other words, the total replenishment lead time usually greatly exceeds the customer order lead time). This is why businesses need to hold inventory of materials or work in progress—because their replenishment lead time is longer than their customer order lead time.

The final lead time to consider brings it all together. This is process lead time and is usually calculated by tracking materials through your process or supply chain. I usually explain it by asking, "If I were to date-stamp a unit of raw material on arrival at your facility, how long, on average, would it take until it left your facility as a finished good?"

This can be extended to encompass the whole supply chain, so perhaps you would track the lead time for a raw material from when it entered your supplier's factory, through their factory, your inbound supply chain, and then through your factories and warehouses and your distribution network, until it got to the end customer. To understand process lead time, you need a tool called a value stream map, which we will describe below.

The common thread of all the measures of lead time in your process—namely, process lead time, order fulfillment lead time, and replenishment lead time (plus work-in-progress replenishment)—is that the longer the lead time, the more inventory you will need to hold *and* the greater the risk of failing to deliver on time and in full. Therefore, a key goal of supply chain managers should be to continually reduce all the lead times in their process.

Takt Time: Keeping Track of Whether You Are Keeping up with Demand

Takt time is the rate of customer demand. It is calculated by dividing the available productive time per day (usually in seconds or minutes) by the average daily demand. Therefore, in an operation working an 8-hour shift with a 1-hour planned break per day, there will be 420 minutes of productive time per day. If that operation produces on average of 210 products per day, the takt time will be 420 divided by 210, or two minutes per product.

I cannot overemphasize the importance of this metric to your supply chain. What it means is that, *on average*, every process in your business, and every supplier, needs to be capable of delivering one product every two minutes. Deliver more, and you will build up inventory. Deliver less, and you will face shortages and let your customer down. Takt time is therefore the yardstick against which you measure every process. Processes that cannot meet takt need additional capacity to speed them up. Processes that go faster than takt should be slowed down to match takt time. Yes, you did read that correctly—*slowed down*. The aim of your process is to meet customer demand, not to ensure that every machine or process goes at maximum speed. By running high-speed machines or simple processes faster than takt time, you create imbalances in your process that will make your delivery performance worse.

Push, Pull, and Flow

Fundamental to understanding the difference between the conventional supply chain approach and the Lean approach is to understand the concepts of push, pull, and flow.

In a conventional supply chain approach, we decide what to manufacturer based on a forecast. Therefore, we anticipate the materials and resources that we expect will be needed by the process and *push* these to the process before production starts. Typically, we use software called material requirements planning (MRP) to plan what materials will be required at each step of our process, looking weeks into the future. Production or shipping will then be scheduled in advanced based on what we expect to sell. Unfortunately, forecasts are often inaccurate, a problem we will discuss more in Chapter 3. As a result, the materials and production we thought we would need often end up not being the ones required. We then need to reschedule production to meet the actual customer demand once we know what that is. To maximize "efficiency," push production usually accumulates demand into batches or "economic order quantities" based on balancing the need to provide long "efficient" production runs and the need to minimize inventory. Doing work in batches is a fundamental part of the DNA of push production.

Lean is built on the concept of *just-in-time*, the idea that each process should only have exactly what it needs in the quantity it needs when it needs it and no more. The ultimate expression of just-in-time is the concept of one-piece flow. You can see one-piece flow on a modern automotive assembly line. Each car flowing along the line is a "batch" of one. The whole range of models will flow along the line at once and, for example, a blue luxury sedan may be followed by a silver SUV and then by a green coupe. Materials are "sequenced in line" to match the sequence of vehicles flowing along the line. One-piece flow is the system of scheduling that provides the lowest level of waste because there is no inventory at all between each step of the production process.

It is not always possible to achieve one-piece flow. For example, a process in the flow may need to stop and start and you may not want to stop every process in the flow every time this happens. When it is not possible to achieve one-piece flow, then a first-in, first-out (FIFO) lane is often used to control the production from one process step to the next. Production flowing into the FIFO lane must be consumed by the downstream process in the sequence that it arrives from the upstream process. As well, the maximum amount of work in progress that can accumulate in a FIFO lane is strictly limited in order to limit the lead time between the two processes. If the inventory in the FIFO lane reaches this limit, then the upstream process must stop. FIFO is a type of flow, because work flows in the same sequence through the process without the need for scheduling.

Sometimes, even a FIFO lane won't work because, for example, two processes operate at different speeds or different working hours. It may be necessary for an upstream process, such as stamping or injection molding, to manufacture batches, or an upstream process may need to be shared by several downstream processes. In a warehouse, an inventory buffer is usually necessary to allow for variation in customer demand. Therefore, in these situations the Lean approach is to use a *pull* system. In a pull system, the upstream process or supplier simply replenishes what the downstream process or warehouse has previously consumed. Frequently, a small signal card (Kanban) will be attached to each container of products or materials, and as each container is sold or consumed, the signal card is returned to the upstream process or supplier, triggering the supply or manufacture of replacement inventory.

In a Lean supply chain, we always aim for one-piece flow. If this is not achievable, then we try to maintain flow and bridge the gap with a FIFO lane. If neither of these options will work, then a pull system is the option we choose. Push production is not part of a Lean supply chain.

Understanding Your Supply Chain with a Value Stream Map

A fundamental principle of Lean thinking is the idea of value and waste. In the Lean methodology, value is an activity that adds value to a product, and for which the customer is willing to pay. Waste is then defined as everything that does not add value. Therefore, we often refer to waste as non-value-added activity. To really understand the full extent of waste in your supply chain, and to find ways of eliminating it, we use a value stream map.

A value stream map is a special type of process map that illustrates the flow of value through your business. It is composed of two interconnected flows:

■ The process flow, which includes all the steps your product flows through in its journey from raw material to delivery to your customer.
■ The information flow, which shows all the communication and data processing steps that trigger the movement of your product through your business. This can include everything from taking the order, to developing and distributing the production plan, to ordering the raw materials.

By including both the process and the information flow, the value stream map helps reveal two important things: where the waste is in your process and why that waste exists.

Creating a value stream map is usually carried out by a cross-functional team, representing all the key functions and subject matter experts engaged in the process. For example, the value stream team for a manufacturing process will usually include production, warehousing, planning, purchasing, sales, and customer service. At the same time, it is important to define the scope of your value stream map—in other words, which group of products you are mapping, and the beginning and ending points of the value stream. At a minimum, your value stream should cover the whole process flow, from receiving to dispatch, within your facility, or "dock to dock," as it is sometimes called.

Before you can draw the map, you need to identify the product family or families that you want to focus on. A "product family" is a group of products that follow a similar process from raw material to finished goods. Typically, these products undergo similar or the same process steps, often on shared equipment. They may involve common materials from common suppliers and will often be sold through a common distribution channel. The idea is to define your product family as broad as makes sense; otherwise, you will find that you have a multiplicity of small product families and a very complex value stream mapping task. In reality, most businesses only have a few key product families (usually less than five) that drive most of the activity in their business. To get started, you need to decide which product family or families you are going to focus on first. My recommendation is to choose the most important ones for your business, as this will have the biggest impact on your business. It is also easier to make your minor products fit the process designed for your main products than vice versa.

Once you have selected the value stream you want to focus on, you need to define the scope of your value stream. Does it need to include your distribution network? Should suppliers and perhaps their suppliers be considered? Or, is it sufficient just to map your own operation? With these things decided, you can then create your current state map, or a map of the process as it stands today, showing both processing and information flows.

To create a current state map, we start by defining the requirements of the customer in terms of volume, product mix, and supply chain setup (lead times, ordering patterns, order quantities, etc.). We then work back from the customer, identifying each supply chain step and, in the case of manufacturing, each step in the manufacturing process. We continue to work backward until we get to the start point we have defined in our scope. We need to put in key metrics at each point of the process, including the capabilities and performance, lead time, and cycle time of each process step. We also need to record inventory at each process step. Transport lead times also need to be included. Once the process flow is complete, we then start with the customer again and map the information flow from the customer placing an order (or providing a forecast) through to the completion of dispatch documentation to ship the goods to the customer, including the process for replenishing materials and scheduling activity in the factory and/or warehouse. Finally, we tie it all together with a "tie line" that calculates the end-to-end lead time for the process.

The current state map will identify the value-added and non-value-added activity (waste) in your process and where it is located. The non-value-added time in your value stream represents the opportunity for you to reduce lead time. Figure 2.2 shows a completed current state map, including the extended supply chain from the factory in China to the customer warehouse in Australia.

To work out how to eliminate the waste that we identify in the current state map, we need to go to the next step of the value stream mapping process—developing a future state map.

The future state map is created by answering the following series of questions about your process:

■ What is the takt time for our process, or the rate of customer demand?
■ What is our finished goods strategy (is it make-to-order or make-to-stock)?
■ Are there processes we can eliminate completely or combine with other processes?
■ Of the remaining processes, how do we connect them to ensure an efficient and reliable flow of products, with a minimum of waste?
■ What is our pacemaker process, or how do we control the rate of production, and decide the production sequence?
■ At what interval, and in what quantity of new demand, are we going to release at the pacemaker (also known as the "pitch interval")?

(These terms will be explained in more detail in subsequent chapters, so if they are unfamiliar, don't worry.)

Once you answer these six questions, you will typically have a radically different model of your process than your current one. You will then

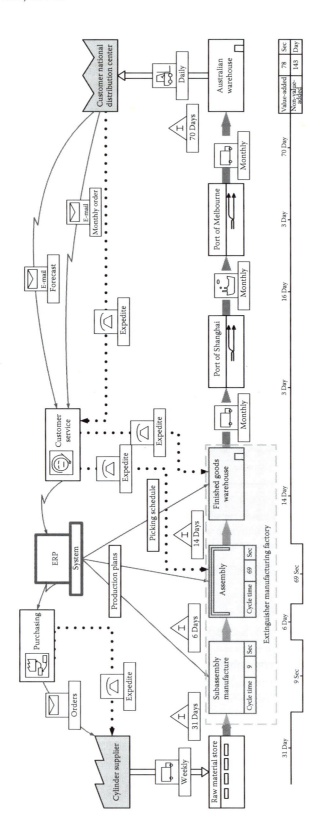

Figure 2.2   Example of a current state value stream map for a fire extinguisher supply chain.

calculate the lead time and other key metrics for your future state, and these will become the goals for your improvement efforts. Figure 2.3 shows the future state map that was developed for the fire extinguisher value stream map in Figure 2.2. From Figure 2.3, you can see that the supply chain now includes many of the concepts discussed in this chapter, including FIFO lanes, pull systems (also known as Kanban systems), and releasing of production at a single point or pacemaker at a regular interval or pitch. In this case, by implementing a Lean supply chain, the lead time was reduced from 143 days to 92 days.

The final step of value stream mapping is to complete an action plan. Usually, this will have a time span of between six and nine months, since longer action plans tend not to be completed. You aren't looking for a perfect future state here. Rather, you want a set of improvements that you can achieve in a relatively short timeframe.

I encourage you to follow this value stream mapping rule:

> *Never draw a current state unless you intend to develop a future state map. Never complete a future state map without developing an action plan to implement it. And never complete an action plan without implementing it!*

This avoids a tendency some companies have to value stream map everything, and ensures that some action will result from making a value stream map.

Once achieved, the future state becomes your new current state, and you can then plan a new set of improvements as your next future state.

This is a very brief introduction to value stream mapping. There are also a number of very good books that will give you a detailed understanding of the technique. It can also be a good idea to get the assistance of an external expert or consultant when you get started with mapping your process. In terms of books, I recommend *Learning to See** by John Shook and Mike Rother as the best book with which to start.

Typically, value stream maps are used to understand the flow of value within an organization. However, your ability to achieve on-time and in-full delivery is often heavily influenced by factors outside your organization. Problems upstream in your supplier base, and downstream in your

---

* Rother, M. and Shook, J. 2003. *Learning to See: Value-Stream Mapping to Create Value and Eliminate Muda*. Brookline, MA: Lean Enterprise Institute.

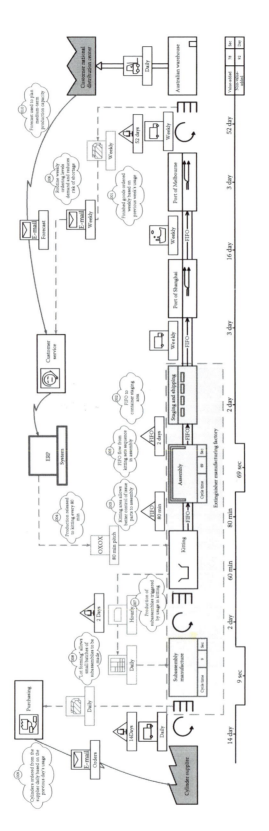

Figure 2.3 Example of a future state value stream map for a fire extinguisher supply chain.

distribution network, can be the deciding factors in whether you deliver an order to your customers on time and in full, or let your customers down. To address these problems, you need to include your suppliers and your distribution network in your value stream. This is called an extended value stream map.

Developing an extended value stream map is best described in the book *Seeing the Whole*,* by Dan Jones and Jim Womack, and I recommend you either get this book or get some expert advice, before embarking on mapping your extended value stream. In an extended value stream, the process is similar to a dock-to-dock value stream. You put together a team representing all the key participants in the value stream, develop a current state map, create a future state map, and then agree on an action plan with a six- to nine-month horizon, while also choosing the level of detail. Initially, you might only map the key supply chain participants as single process steps within the flow, as shown in Figure 2.4. As you can see, this is the fire extinguisher supply chain shown in Figure 2.3, but in this case, the extinguisher factory is shown as an external supplier with a single icon. As well, you can see that the supply chain has been extended beyond the national distribution center to take in the full distribution chain to the end customer. This kind of extended value stream will show you where the waste is located in the overall value stream, and how the various supply chain participants connect with one another. This can be very useful in a distribution network, in which the various supply chain participants are warehouses, and do not, as a result, add value within their operations.

Later, you might want to drill down and complete a dock-to-dock value stream within some or all the supply chain partners, as we have done in Figure 2.3. This will probably start with your own operation, but it can be useful to also complete a dock-to-dock value stream within your key suppliers' operations, if they will let you. This requires a deep relationship and a lot of trust with your supplier.

Summary

To deliver on time and in full to your customers, you need to understand your supply chain, and identify the key limitations and constraints that

---

* Jones, D. and Womack, J. 2011. *Seeing the Whole Value Stream.* Brookline, MA: Lean Enterprise Institute.

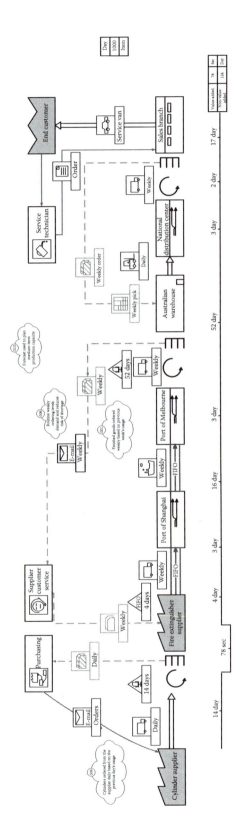

Figure 2.4 Example of a simplified future state value stream map for the extended supply chain for fire extinguishers.

impact your performance. In this chapter, I have introduced a number of concepts you need to understand before you can really make sense of what is happening in your supply chain. I have also provided you with a brief overview of the most powerful supply chain analysis tool, the value stream map. This understanding of your supply chain is the first step toward learning why your business struggles to deliver production on time and in full, and the first step toward finding a solution.

We will now start to examine in more detail the elements of your supply chain that most impact your ability to deliver to your customers what they need on time and in full, starting with that most vexed of all supply chain topics, forecasting.

Key Points in Chapter 2

To improve on-time, in-full delivery in your business, you need to understand your supply chain and how the various elements of that supply chain contribute to your ultimate delivery performance.

A supply chain is the series of steps and processes by which value is added to a product, and through which it is delivered to an end customer.

Critical concepts to understand in the supply chain include

- Lead times, including lead time from order to delivery, as well as the lead time to replenish materials and the overall lead time to process products in your facility. The longer the lead time, the harder it usually is to consistently deliver reliably to customers.
- Takt time, the average rate of customer demand. Every step in the supply chain needs to be able to deliver at takt time in order to consistently meet your customers' demands.
- Traditional supply chains, which "push" products and materials to meet forecast demand. The push approach is prone to frequent delivery failure because forecasts are usually inaccurate. Lean supply chains either "flow" products in a continuous stream to meet that demand or "pull" products or materials to replenish those that have been sold or consumed.
- Value stream map, a highly effective way to understand how value and waste is created in your supply chain. The future state value stream map will enable you to apply logical tools to develop a new supply chain that will deliver shorter lead times and improved delivery to customers.

Chapter 3

Understanding the Future—The Mystery of Forecasting

What You Will Learn in This Chapter

- *The value and limitations of forecasting*
- *The right level and frequency to forecast your demand*
- *What you should use a forecast for and what you should not use it for*
- *The role of a forecast in planning the supply of materials*
- *How to develop and maintain a rolling annual forecast*

The Promise of Forecasting

The greatest challenge in delivering our products on time and in full is that we do not know exactly what our customer will need and when they will need it. Most businesses take time to respond to changes in customer demand. This is because of lead times in production and lead times from their suppliers. For example, if our products and materials have a replenishment lead time of 90 days, and the customer significantly increases their forecast demand for next month, then it is likely that we will face shortages and expediting if we are to supply that customer demand. Alternatively, if we choose to have more inventory to allow for an unexpected *increase* in demand and that demand actually *decreases*, then we are likely to be left with a warehouse full of excess stock.

Ideally, we would negotiate with our customer to make them give us enough lead time to source and/or manufacture their products. However, as we learned in Chapter 2, total replenishment lead times are often measured in months, and few customers are prepared to wait that long (and even when they are, pesky competitors are always promising shorter lead times). It seems like an impossible conundrum—customers want our products in a lead time shorter than our business and our supply chain can achieve.

But what if we could accurately predict what our customers would order sufficiently far in advance that we could have time to obtain materials and manufacture the goods. If we could do that, then delivering on time and in full would be easy, because when the customer placed their order, we would already have the goods available, ready to deliver. This is the alluring promise of forecasting, and literally billions have been spent on software, computer power, and demand management specialists around the world trying to fulfill that promise.

Can We Tell the Future?

One of the great desires of humans over the millennia is the ability to forecast the future. We have looked to the stars, the gods, crystal balls, tea leaves, our palms, and tarot cards to tell us what will happen to us in the future. Today, we look to software to tell us the future, but the reality remains—we cannot predict the future. All we can do is approximate it.

Once upon a time, I worked in a business that was very committed to the success of its enterprise resource planning* (ERP) software package. We expended a lot of energy measuring forecast accuracy. This was (in our case) the number of products where the actual demand in a given month fell within ±30% of the forecast demand. This means that the actual demand could be anywhere between 70% and 130% of the forecast demand, and we still considered that to be an accurate forecast. We put a lot of effort into

---

* An ERP is a business information system that connects the day-to-day operations of a business with its accounts. ERP systems typically handle the transactions associated with order fulfillment, including sales order processing, shop floor control, inventory management, and purchasing. Most ERP systems have material requirements planning functionality built in, which allows for production and purchasing of products and materials to be planned based on a forecast. Chapter 10 provides more detail about ERP systems.

"demand management," used sophisticated analytical software, and engaged in much brow beating of customers to provide an accurate forecast (including reporting back to customers when they "got it wrong"). Through all this, we managed to get our forecast accuracy up to 80% on a one-month horizon. What this meant was that the forecast we finalized at the end of each month's sales and operations planning cycle* was accurate for the following month. In other words, we had an 80% chance that the forecast we worked out on June 20 would fall somewhere between 70% and 130% of actual July demand. Notwithstanding the fact that it was not particularly useful to know that demand would be in a range between 70% and 130%, our production lead time was closer to two months and the raw material lead time on top of that was often three months or more. This meant that for a forecast to be much use for planning production in July, we would need to have made it back in February. Even our three-month forecast accuracy was below 50%, so our chances of making a meaningful prediction of demand five months out was effectively zero. In summary, all our hard work in creating a forecast every month was essentially useless.

Forecasting and the Weather

To understand the problems of forecasting, it is useful to think about the weather. Some of the world's most powerful computers are used to forecast the weather, but even then there are some severe limitations. Let's say it is October and we are trying to predict the weather in New York City in January. There is some information we would be able to predict. January is likely to be colder than October, and there would be a good chance of snow. This is useful information as it might affect some long-range decisions, like what clothes we buy and when we plan to take our holidays. But what about the weather in New York on the first of January? Even the best forecaster with the most powerful supercomputer would hesitate to give anything more than a broad range of outcomes for the weather on a specific day three months in the future. Even if we widened the time horizon to the first week of January, providing an accurate forecast that far out is almost impossible.

The point here is that the value of forecasts depends on the time horizon and the level of detail that you attempt to forecast. Using a forecast of limited accuracy to decide what products to make on a given week or,

---

* More about sales and operations planning in Chapter 4.

worse, a given day, three or more months in advance, is likely to mean that you will be making the wrong product in the wrong quantities at the wrong time to meet your customers' needs.

Importance of Significance

Most people in manufacturing have some form of science or math training. Therefore, we will have learned about the concept of significance in measurement. We all learned this when we first got calculators that could calculate to 10 decimal places. I think most of us can remember getting a metaphorical rap over the knuckles from our science teacher when we subtracted two similar numbers to get a result to the third decimal place, when, in fact, the measurement error was greater than the difference we had calculated. Likewise, every day we read polls in the newspaper and often ignore the statement that the "margin for error is 3%." Computers will generate for us highly detailed tables of forecast data down to the expected demand of individual products on individual days, but the forecast error at this level will be so great as to make this impressive list of numbers meaningless. We therefore need to ensure that we are forecasting at a level of detail where the forecast error is not so large as to make the numbers meaningless. We need to consider the "significance" of the forecast data.

Building a Forecast

There is a huge body of literature, many PhDs, and mountains of software written for forecasting demand; however, it is best to start from the simplest point.

The best predictor of what you are going to sell next month (all other things being equal) is what you sold in the corresponding month last year.

In our experience, it is sufficient to forecast for 12 months at monthly intervals. That will give you an indication of seasonality, as well as trends throughout the year (e.g., the rate at which your sales are growing).

For high-level planning of your operation, monthly sales history is ideal. The decisions you are going to make with this data are to determine the level of assets, people, capacity, and materials you require. These are medium-term decisions, not week-to-week decisions. *The shorter the time interval (or time bucket) you choose, the less accurate the forecast will be.* That is because of the averaging effect you get when aggregating the data from days to weeks to months.

Time interval is one limiting factor on forecasts; the other is the level of the forecast. This is best illustrated by an example:

Our customer was a manufacturer of architectural coatings (house paint). They sold around 400 products. However, these products were manufactured from around 90 basic paint formulations. This is because a single paint product was typically packaged in multiple pack variants—ranging from 500 ml sample pots to 15l buckets. The 90 base products were manufactured in four main dispersing mixers. Forecasting 400 products individually was almost impossible. Forecasting demand for the 90 base products was much easier, and forecasting demand on the four dispersers easier still. Forecasts of the total monthly throughput of the whole factory were usually fairly accurate. Therefore, the accuracy of the forecast created depended on the level of the forecast—whether it was individual products, base formulations, dispersing lines, or the whole factory. The higher the level, the greater the accuracy of the forecast that can be created.

Usually, it is best to forecast at the level of a whole value stream. In Chapter 2, we talked about takt time as a measure of customer demand. We recommend you develop a simple overall measure of output for your business that can be used to determine the takt time. It could be orders, jobs, tons, units, batches, pallets, or whatever other measure you choose. The important thing is that the measure is a good indicator of the level of business activity in your business.

For example, when I took over as operations director of a large automotive coatings factory, the main measure of demand was liters. The problem was that demand of 100,000 L could represent five batches of 20,000 L each or 100 batches of 1,000 L each. The actual level of activity in the factory (how busy we were) was more closely related to the number of batches we had to make than the number of liters we had to make. This was because the amount of time and effort involved in making a large batch was pretty similar to those of a small batch. We therefore changed the key output measure that we used from number of liters to number of batches.

Table 3.1   Monthly Forecast for a House Paint Factory

Forecast Demand (batches)	Jan	Feb	Mar	Apr	May	Jun	Jul	Aug	Sep	Oct	Nov	Dec
Disperser 1	15	20	18	15	9	9	7	17	23	25	25	14
Disperser 2	5	7	6	5	3	3	2	6	8	9	8	4
Disperser 3	29	41	38	28	20	18	15	35	44	53	51	25
Disperser 4	57	83	74	59	40	35	28	68	92	100	98	52

The monthly forecast needs to be expressed in the output measure you choose. As a result, your forecast can be as simple as the example shown in Table 3.1.

Compared with the massive spreadsheets and computer reports that many companies call their forecast, Table 3.1 might seem ridiculously simple. However, it provides critical information in terms of the required rate of production for each value stream and can allow for planning of capacity and labor requirements through the year. It allows us to calculate the takt time in terms of minutes per batch for each production line so that we can balance our production flow. It shows seasonality so you can see that demand is lowest in the Australian winter as few people paint their houses in winter (May to July) and peaks in the spring (October and November) as paint stores stock up for the summer painting "season." This is all vital information and allowed this company to plan its labor and adjust its raw material and finished goods inventory levels through the year to match this demand cycle. However, the week-to-week and day-to-day replenishment of the warehouse was triggered through that simple Lean pull system introduced in Chapter 2 and discussed in more detail later in this book.

Forecasting Raw Material Requirements

Unless the bills of materials for your product are very simple (which they are not in paint manufacture), a simple forecast such as the one above does not appear very useful for forecasting raw material demand. This is important because the reason that we are often doing the forecast is to assist our suppliers by predicting our requirements for materials. For this reason, many companies use their ERP software to break down the forecast demand into forecasts for individual materials that they then provide to their suppliers. These forecasts look very impressive and are intended to help the supplier ensure that they can reliably meet their customer's demand. Having been the recipient of many such forecasts from customers, I would suggest that they often are more a source of confusion than assistance.

*We worked with a supplier of packaging to the consumer electronics industry in South China. Their major customer communicated their requirements in four different ways—a rolling 52-week forecast, a monthly order, a weekly shipment schedule, and the daily call-ups, which triggered the actual delivery of packaging to the customer. We analyzed all this information and found that there was zero statistical correlation between the four levels of forecast. That is, what the customer actually required on a particular day or week bore **no resemblance whatsoever** to what had been predicted in the weekly shipping schedule, the monthly order, or even the rolling weekly forecast. The forecasts were worse than useless because the packaging company put a lot of effort into trying to plan production according to the weekly forecast, and then had to change production schedules and expedite production when what their customer actually required bore no resemblance between what had been forecasted and made.*

So how do we help suppliers to deliver us the right stuff when we need it so we can deliver the right stuff to our customers when they need it? From a forecasting perspective, the first question we need to ask is, "What does the supplier need from a forecast?" For local suppliers, with a short lead time, a forecast may not be needed at all. This is especially the case if they are supplying you from their stock with a product where your demand is only a small part of the total demand for that product. Even for many other products where the supplier has to make your product to order, the lead time will be less than a month. For these items, a pull system or Kanban system will be the best option and a forecast is not necessary beyond an indication of your overall level of activity (such as the forecast in Table 3.1).

Once you eliminate suppliers who do not need a forecast from you, you will narrow down your requirement for supplier forecasts to a few critical suppliers of long-lead-time items.

It is important to remember what we are trying to achieve with the forecasts you give to your suppliers. Your material forecast is not there to control what the customer supplies to you and when. Instead, the purpose of a monthly material forecast is to provide suppliers with an indication of your high-level expected overall demand. This will enable them to plan their own capacity and source their own materials. This ensures that when your real demand comes in the form of orders or Kanban pull signals, the suppliers are able to supply on time.

Low-Volume Products and Materials

Another reason I have seen companies insist on using forecast-driven replenishment (push process) is to manage low-usage products or materials. This is fundamentally illogical. In fact, the low and infrequent usage of these items makes a forecast even more difficult to calculate, and the forecast generated by your software system will be even less accurate than that generated for high-volume items. For low-usage items, you need to accept that either you will have to carry a higher level of inventory (in days' cover) of these items or you and your customers will have to accept the need to only order these items when required. Remember that the value of inventory associated with a higher level of stock cover of these items will be low because the usage of these items is low. However, regular monitoring is needed to make sure that the low-volume item does not become a "no-volume item" (i.e., obsolete) and you get struck with stock you cannot sell. Often, it is worth regularly challenging your product management team to ask them whether the low-volume items are really required or can they be phased out.

Generating the Forecast

Hopefully, you will now agree that all you need is a simply monthly forecast at a fairly high level to plan your business. But how do you generate this forecast? Here are some simple steps to help you create a useful monthly forecast for your business without the need for advanced software or a whole demand management team.

The important point to remember when generating a forecast is that people are not very good at forecasting the future. Therefore, it is best to build your forecast based on facts rather than guesswork.

Start with your previous year's actual sales history. Ask yourself, "What will be different about next year compared with this year?" Stick to what you know and be specific. Work out what your historical annual growth rate has been. Is there any reason it will be different next year? If not, apply the forecasted growth rate based on the previous year's data. Remember that sales on month 1 of the new financial year will not suddenly increase by 5% just because you budgeted for a 5% increase. Growth is likely to be more gradual through the year. Again, there are a lot of models to choose from, but I think a simple linear model of growth is the most sensible, as you are unlikely to have sufficient information to predict anything else with any degree of accuracy 12 months out.

What seasonal trends did you see last year? For example, soft drink sales are much higher in the summer. Was last year a normal season, or should you consider more past seasons to forecast an average?

Were there any demand spikes (such as promotions) that occurred last year but will not occur this year? If so, remove their influence from the forecast.

Likewise, are you expecting any one-off demand spikes this year that did not occur last year? How much are you expecting to sell during those spikes? Factor them into the forecast.

Are there products that you sold last year that will not be sold next year? If so, will they be phased out completely or replaced by new products? Will the sales of the new products be the same, more, or less than the former products? If sales levels are changing, why are they changing? What are those assumptions based on?

Make sure that you document all the assumptions that you build into the forecast.

Remember, we are only trying to forecast total demand at the value stream level. Do not worry about every single product—just the ones that represent a significant proportion of the demand on the value stream.

Are there new products that will be introduced in the forecasted year? What quantities do you expect to sell of those products? Why do you expect to sell that much? What are the assumptions? Where will those sales come from? At the expense of your competitors? If so, how will the competitors respond and how might that affect your forecast?

Try Sensitivity Analysis

It is a good idea to do some contingency planning. Ask hypothetical questions such as, what is the highest level of sales you realistically might expect to achieve? Under what circumstances are you likely to achieve those sales levels? As always, check your assumptions. What would the sales forecast look like under those assumptions?

Another factor to consider is, what is the realistic worst-case scenario for sales? Under what circumstances would you be likely to achieve this? What would the sales forecast look like in this scenario?

Forecasting Tools

For most businesses, it is possible to create a perfectly adequate forecast using Microsoft Excel. However, there are a number of commercially available forecasting tools that can assist you to create a forecast. These tools vary in complexity and cost, and I recommend you evaluate a few to determine one that will meet the particular needs of your business. These tools will import sales history, either from your ERP system or a spreadsheet, and can apply a range of analytical tools to identify and model seasonality, trends, and other factors and then export the finished sales forecast directly back into your ERP or spreadsheet.

There is a trap in using forecasting software. The software will be able to generate a forecast for every single product you manufacture, right down to the individual stock keeping unit (SKU) and at a weekly level. Such a forecast will look really impressive and look like valuable data. However, remember what I said earlier in the chapter: weekly forecasts down to the SKU level months into the future are likely to be completely inaccurate, no matter how good your forecasting tool is.

I would argue that creating a forecast for total demand on a value stream (like Table 3.1) at the monthly level is a fairly simple exercise that can be handled by most competent users of Excel without the need for advanced forecasting software.

Demand Management: Maintaining the Forecast

Creating your first forecast is challenging and rewarding. However, once you have your first 12 months of expected sales data, do not expect the process to stop there. Forecasts need to be maintained to be useful, as the factors that impact them change over time.

Typically, the forecast maintenance or demand management process happens every month. A month has gone by, so the forecast will need to be extended out by 1 month to maintain the 12-month time horizon.

Then the focus should be on what has changed since last month. Focus on major changes, such as new promotions, new product launches, product deletions, or major changes in the market. It is easy to turn the monthly forecasting process into a laborious line-by-line recasting of the forecast. However, as I said above, the forecast is only an estimate of what might happen, and a rough estimate at that, so trying to finesse the data is fairly pointless.

A difficult issue can be new product development. You know the product is coming, but you don't know how well it will sell or perhaps even what it will be called. In this case, you may choose to insert a line in your forecast for the new product demand so that you lock in the production capacity, but do not necessarily trigger ordering of materials.

By maintaining a monthly update, you will soon start to learn what changes need to be specifically incorporated into the forecast and which ones are not significant. You will also find the most meaningful level to forecast at. In Chapter 4, we will explain sales and operations planning, a structured approach to reviewing your business's demand, and its ability to supply over a 12- to 18-month time horizon.

Key Points in Chapter 3

Traditional push approaches to supply chain management are based on using a forecast to determine future requirements for products and materials in order to meet future customer demand. This model suffers because forecasts are inherently inaccurate, because humans cannot predict the future.

- The accuracy of a forecast is impacted by three parameters:
    - The length of the forecast: The further you try to forecast into the future, the less accurate the forecast will be.
    - The time interval being forecasted: Forecasting a larger time interval will give a more accurate result than a shorter time interval. Therefore, it is much easier to forecast monthly demand than weekly or daily demand.
    - The level of the forecast: Accurately forecasting demand for every individual product is much harder than forecasting product families or value streams.

■ Taking into account these factors, the most useful forecast is a simple monthly forecast of demand for the whole value stream extended out for 12 months. This forecast allows for long-run planning of resources and materials, but pull systems should be used for day-to-day and week-to-week replenishment.

■ Forecasting tools can be used to automate generation of the 12-month forecast, but a simple forecast can usually be created on a spreadsheet.

■ A forecast should start with sales history (what you sold last year), and then you can overlay known changes, such as growth trends, seasonality, promotions, and known product introductions and deletions.

■ You should review and adjust your forecast monthly, adding an additional month to the end of the 12-month forecast and adjusting for known and significant changes in demand.

■ Ideally, the monthly forecast review should form part of the sales and operations planning process that I will explain in Chapter 4.

Chapter 4

Can We Do It? Effective Sales and Operations Planning

What You Will Learn in This Chapter

- *Why sales and operations planning is an important tool to ensure your business can deliver on time and in full to its customers*
- *How to develop simple tools for understanding production capacity*
- *The difference between cycle time and takt time and why it matters for capacity planning*
- *The importance of understanding the capacity of your bottleneck*
- *The basics of implementing a sales and operations planning process in your business*
- *The key elements of a sales and operations planning process*
- *How to set up a simple sales and operations planning process in your business*

Matching Capacity to Demand: The Foundation for On-Time Delivery

In Chapter 2, you will have identified some fundamental aspects of your supply chain, including the idea of matching your output to the rate of customer demand or takt time. Fundamental to Lean thinking is the idea of level production, where factories and supply chains run best when the output of every step is maintained at a constant level rate, equal to takt time.

However, from Chapter 3 you will have developed a simple, high-level monthly forecast for your business, which will most likely show that customer demand will vary throughout the year. This implies that demand is in fact not constant through the year and actually varies from month to month and season to season.

In Figure 4.1, you can see that forecast demand for paint (measured in batches per month) varies greatly over the year. The average is 65 batches per month, but in July demand drops to 28 batches, while in October it peaks at 100 batches.

The question therefore is how to respond to this variation? If you do not respond, then the inevitable result is that you will let customers down and run out of stock in the peak months and be overstocked in the quiet months.

So what is the best way to respond to this demand variation? Should you try to speed up or slow down the rate of production to match demand, increase or reduce working hours (while keeping the rate of production constant), increase inventory buffers to dampen out the variation, or a combination of all three? Importantly, all three of these options involve costs and take time and planning to execute. Therefore, apart from developing a forecast 12 months in advance, there is a need to plan how the organization will supply that demand well in advance as well. This process of planning

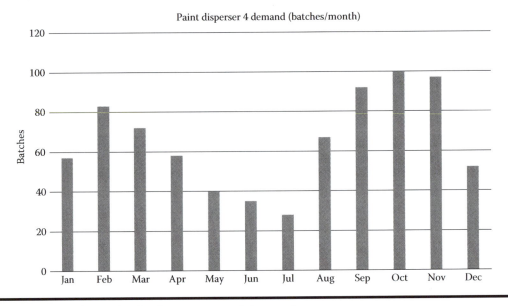

Figure 4.1 Chart of paint factory annual demand.

supply and demand in the future is called sales and operations planning (S&OP).

Like many aspects of supply chain, supply chain experts and consultants have made S&OP into a very complex and labor-intensive process with many meetings every month and a large deck of metrics and reports to present. As a result, many organizations, particularly smaller organizations, see S&OP as not for them or something they will get around to once they "get the basics right." In fact, I would suggest that a rudimentary S&OP process *is* one of the basic elements of getting the supply chain right. There is no point creating a forecast if you do not plan well in advance how your organization will respond to that forecast. Also, replenishment lead times are typically much longer than customer order lead times. As a result, you must take action well before expected changes in demand if you are to successfully respond to those changes and continue to deliver on time, in full. In this chapter, we want to focus on the basics of S&OP—an understanding of your organization's ability to meet its expected future demand. The first step toward that is understanding the capacity of your factory, distribution network, and supply chain.

To determine what you can make, you need to know what the capacity of your process (let's call it your value stream) is. There are lots of different ways to build a capacity model, but as I have emphasized several times already, the key is not to overcomplicate things. If you are testing the limits of Excel's processing capability or investing thousands in specialized software, you have probably gone too far.

Cycle Time and Takt Time: Developing a Simple Rough-Cut Capacity Model

To understand capacity, you need to understand the difference between cycle time and takt time. In Chapter 2, we explained takt time as the average rate of customer demand. It is important to remember that takt time is purely a function of sales; it is not dependent on the capabilities of your factory or suppliers' factories.

On the other hand, cycle time is the rate of output that your machine or process can achieve on average. The cycle time is unrelated to sales and forecasts—it is a measure of what your process can achieve. Cycle time determines your capacity, which is how much product we can manufacture over a given period of time. The key therefore is making sure that the capacity (what the process can achieve) is always greater than the demand. In practice, this means that the cycle time of every process must be less than the takt time required for that process. If capacity is less than forecast demand, you will fall further and further behind and let your customers down.

If you are a distribution business and not a manufacturer, this concept is still important. Your key suppliers need to be able to meet takt time, and your own internal office and warehouse processes need to be set up to ensure that their cycle times are equal to or lower than takt time.

For example, in the case of our process in Figure 4.1, the time it takes an operator to prepare and disperse a batch on Disperser 4 might be on average 120 minutes. Based on an 8-hour shift (420 working minutes) and 20 working days per month, the capacity on the disperser will be 70 batches per month. We need to compare this with our forecast demand. We plot the monthly capacity against our demand to produce a very simple capacity model in Figure 4.2. As you can see in the low months of May to July, capacity greatly exceeds demand, while in the peak months of September to November, demand outstrips the capacity. The business therefore needs to make decisions about how to respond to these capacity gaps in order to

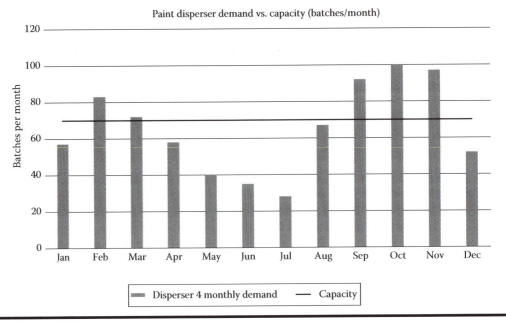

Figure 4.2 Comparison between demand and capacity time for paint factory value stream.

ensure that customers can obtain the product they need on time and in full all year.

For many processes, this is the only capacity model you will need. It highlights the key capacity challenges through the year and enables the business to make decisions to respond to those challenges. In fact, in a large industrial coatings factory I managed, we used this exact method to calculate capacity across four value streams and thousands of individual products. By simply balancing the demand in batches to our capacity to produce batches, we were able to effectively manage seasonal and promotional demand swings and achieve record levels of on-time, in-full delivery.

The keys to using a simple model like this are

- A common unit of measure that is a good indicator of the level of activity across the product range. For many processes, mix variations such as differing cycle times for different products and differing batch sizes will average out over time. This enables a single output measure to be used across all products.
- Different value streams that are largely independent of each other. Where you have assets that are shared across different value streams, you need to consider the capacity loading on these assets in total for all value streams rather than individually.
- Processes are largely people driven—meaning the output is determined by the pace of work maintained by people working in the process—rather than machine driven.

More Advanced Capacity Models

Unfortunately, not every process can use a capacity model as simple as the one I have shown for the paint manufacturing process. This is the case for most machine-driven processes. With machine-driven processes, the rate of output is determined by the cycle time of the machine and other factors, such as loading time, setup time, and average planned and unplanned downtime. For example, computer numerically controlled (CNC) machining is usually machine driven (although manual machining is people driven). Injection molding and other plastics processes are also machine driven. For machine-driven processes, capacity is limited by the capacity of the machines. This means that the maximum number of products that can be produced equals the operating time divided by the cycle time and adjusted for setup time, loading time, and other downtime. You may say that in a "Lean" world, we should not allow for breakdowns or unplanned delays; however, for capacity modeling we need to understand the *actual* demonstrated capacity of the machine. Otherwise, our plan will be too optimistic and customers will be let down. Of course, we are always trying to improve efficiency, reduce setup times, and remove unplanned downtime, but for the purposes of capacity planning, we need to face current reality and plan accordingly. Since machines run a diverse range of products and batch sizes, capacity usually needs to be calculated taking into account those factors.

Despite this, a capacity model need not be excessively complicated.

The example in Table 4.1 is actual data for an injection molding department. It provides a simple model of whether the plant can meet expected customer demand.

Another type of forecast model is the machine capacity sheet shown in Table 4.2.

This shows the capacity loading for a machining center taking into account the key parameters, such as cycle time, loading time, changeover time, and efficiency.

Only Analyze Capacity at the Bottleneck Process

Completing this type of analysis for every machine or work center in your process would be a bit exhausting. However, we usually can focus on just understanding the capacity at the bottleneck process in our value stream. The bottleneck process is the process with the longest cycle time or lowest available capacity. Figure 4.3 shows the steps in our process highlighting the bottleneck. As can be seen, the bottleneck is the dispersion process, and the graph shows that this process cannot meet the required average rate of demand of 65 batches per month, so actions will need to be taken to reduce the cycle time of dispersion in order to ensure that the expected demand can be met. This might become the focus of a continuous improvement project, or it may be necessary to invest in new technology or additional capacity.

Since all other processes have greater capacity than the bottleneck, if we can demonstrate that the bottleneck can meet expected demand, then all the other processes will be able to meet it. If you are not sure which process is your bottleneck or think your bottleneck may have moved to another process, it may be worthwhile to analyze capacity occasionally for these other

Table 4.1 Capacity Model for Injection Molding

Parts Description	Machine Number	Number of Cavities per Tool	Annual Output	Average Weekly Usage	Cycle Time (sec)	Time to Make Weekly Usage at 100% Efficiency (h)	Run Time Allowing for Actual Efficiency (90%)	Changeover Time (min)	Total Run Time per Week per Part (h)	Cumulative Run Time (h)	% Loading over 7 Days
Red skirt tall	1	1	54,080	1,040	50	14	16	60	17	17	10%
Blue skirt tall	1	1	218,400	4,200	55	64	71	60	72	89	53%
Green skirt tall	1	1	104,520	2,010	55	31	34	60	35	124	74%
Black handle	1	4	291,200	5,600	30	12	13	60	14	138	82%
Green nozzle	1	2	60,320	1,160	30	5	5	60	6	145	86%
Blue nozzle	1	2	260,000	5,000	20	14	15	60	16	161	96%
Red nozzle	1	2	57,200	1,100	20	3	3	60	4	166	99%

Table 4.2 Example of a Machine Capacity Chart

Manager	Supervisor	Production Capacity Sheet	Line Name	Machine Number	Date	Group
				Machine Name		Name
			Interval Operating Time	Description 2400	Current Output Person/Day	Pieces
				Tools		Remarks

Step No.	Part Number and Name	Quantity	C/O Time	Load Time	Base Time — Manual Time	Base Time — Machine Time	Base Time — Cycle Time Complete	Tools — Change Frequency	Tools — Time to Change	Processing Time	Remarks
1	Part ABC1 Major customer spindle	18	18	2	40	32	47	5	15	918	
	Part ABC2										
	Part ABC3										
	Part ABC4										
	Part ABC5										
	Part ABC6										
		0	0	0	0	0	0	0	0	0	
Totals		18	18	2	40	32	47	5	15	918	

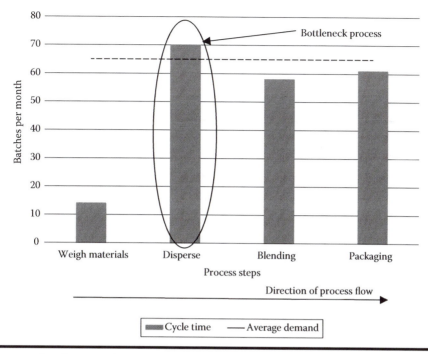

Figure 4.3   Simple capacity model showing the bottleneck for the paint manufacturing example.

processes. Also, if your product mix has changed significantly, then this may cause a different process to be a bottleneck, and again, capacity analysis of the other processes may be needed. However, normally this will be only a one-off exercise, whereas updating the capacity model for your bottleneck process needs to be part of your regular monthly S&OP cycle.

Sales and Operations Planning Process

Many people make S&OP processes very complex with many meetings and complex analysis of huge amounts of data. As I explained in Chapter 3, such analysis may look impressive and may provide some a false sense of security to the creators of that data, but the inherent limitations of forecasting mean that forecasting down to the product level and weekly or daily intervals is likely to be so inaccurate as to be meaningless. Therefore, much of the detailed number crunching involved in S&OP processes is a waste of time because it is built on an assumption that such a detailed forecast is meaningful, which it is not. If we start with a simple, high-level forecast, then our S&OP process can also be quite simple. Figure 4.4 shows an example of a

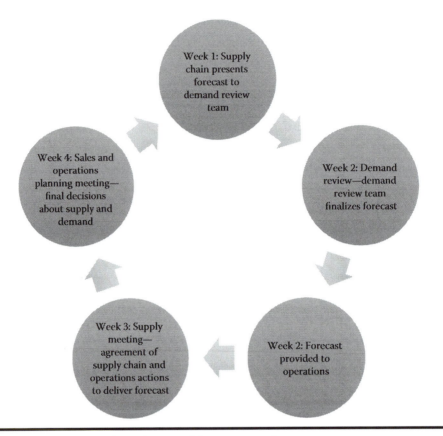

Figure 4.4   Typical timeline of a monthly S&OP cycle.

simple S&OP cycle. There are in fact only three main elements of an effective S&OP process:

1. Demand review: As explained in Chapter 3, this means reviewing the existing forecast, extending it by one month, and adjusting the other months to reflect any new information provided by the sales team. Importantly, the demand review should be "unconstrained." That usually means that the operations and supply chain team are not involved in developing the updated forecast lest they inject bias to reflect their capacity and capabilities. They will get their turn at the next step of the process.

2. Supply review: Once the forecast is complete, it is provided to the operations and supply chain team. Their job is to determine whether the forecast demand can be met with existing resources. When the required demand exceeds what can be delivered, the supply chain team will identify what actions need to be taken to meet the expected demand.

This might include extending working hours with overtime or additional staff, outsourcing some production, finding additional suppliers (if the current ones cannot keep up), or sourcing additional production capacity. Alternatively, if capacity exceeds demand, it might also mean reducing working hours or winding back on suppliers and inventory levels.

3. S&OP meeting: This final meeting is attended by the senior management in the business and is a decision-making meeting. The demand management team present the forecast and the assumptions behind the forecast. The supply chain and operations team then present what actions (if any) are needed to meet the forecast demand. Senior management need to be satisfied that the forecast makes sense, and then need to decide whether the changes to resources recommended by the supply chain and operations team can be supported by the business. It might be necessary for the business to fund additional working capital or fixed capital or employ additional staff (or lay off staff). These decisions need senior leadership approval. If such approval is not given, then decisions need to be made about how the forecast demand will be met. This might lead to portfolio decisions to exit market segments or products in the case of increasing demand. Alternatively, there might be a need to enter new markets or discount products to counter a drop in demand.

As can be seen, the decisions made at that S&OP meeting are not short-term decisions. A common mistake of many organizations is to focus S&OP on the coming month. In fact, there is little the organization can do to influence supply and demand one month out. The focus of S&OP needs to be on the whole planning horizon, which is usually between 12 and 24 months into the future.

Demand Review

Typically, the demand review will be led by the demand manager. This is the person responsible for developing and maintaining the forecast. In large organizations, this is a full-time role, but in smaller organizations, it may be part-time. Many organizations will see demand management as a sales function; however, it makes a lot of sense to place the responsibility for developing the forecast outside sales. Sales teams tend to inject bias into

Table 4.3 Inputs and Outputs for a Demand Review

Inputs	Outputs
Latest 12- to 24-month forecast (prepared in the previous S&OP cycle) Expected seasonal trends Expected sales growth Planned promotional activity Timing of planned product introductions Timing of planned product phase-out Intelligence on competitor activity and other external factors	Forecast demand by value stream for 12–24 months into the future Forecast demand for key raw material suppliers Key assumptions made in the development of the forecast Key risks and opportunities in the forecast period

forecasts. For example, where the sales team lacks confidence in operations' ability to supply, they may bias the forecast upward. On the other hand, the need to demonstrate that they have "overachieved" for the purposes of sales bonuses may bias forecasts downward. It is better that the ultimate responsibility for forecasting sits within the supply chain team. Sales and marketing have a crucial role in providing intelligence about changes in the market and changes in the product range, but an independent forecaster will ensure that biases are avoided. Sometimes two rounds of demand review meetings are required. An initial meeting between the demand manager and sales and marketing team will present the current forecast and provide sales and marketing with the opportunity to notify the demand manager of any expected changes to demand. The demand manager will then update the forecast, and then a second demand review meeting will be held to sign off the final forecast before submission to operations. The key elements of the demand review are shown in Table 4.3.

Supply Review

The supply review needs to involve the supply chain, purchasing, and operations functions. Again, it should be led by the supply chain to avoid bias (it is usually led by the supply chain manager). The forecast is input into the capacity model, and then operations provides input as to the implications of the forecast capacity loadings. For example, will additional shifts be needed, will production be needed on weekends, or are additional machines required? Again, this may be a two-step process, with the first step to present the forecast and the second to review the capacity plan and the key operational changes arising from it (Table 4.4).

Table 4.4 Inputs and Outputs for Supply Review

Inputs	Outputs
Updated forecast (from demand review) "Raw" capacity model with new forecast but last month's capacity assumptions Intelligence of activities and issues in the factory likely to impact capacity (such as planned downtime or public holidays) Backlog of demand uncompleted from previous periods	Updated 12- to 24-month capacity model matching updated forecast and showing capacity loading over forecast period Key changes and resources required to meet updated forecast (compared to previous forecast), e.g., changes to labor, working hours, machine capacity, and outsourcing Key assumptions made in the development of the capacity model Key risks and opportunities in the forecast period

Sales and Operations Planning Meeting

Finally, the S&OP meeting should involve the senior functional managers within the business, usually including the CEO or general manager. The supply chain manager should have circulated a briefing paper prior to the meeting outlining the demand and supply situation and the key decisions that need to be made at the S&OP meeting. That way, the meeting can be tightly focused, decisions can be made during the meeting, and the time of the meeting can be kept to around one hour. The output of the S&OP meeting will be a series of actions that will need to be implemented by the supply chain and operations teams to ensure that the demand requirements can be met and that the organization can continue to achieve on-time, in-full delivery in the future.

In many organizations, the S&OP meeting often reviews the previous month's actual performance and highlights corrective actions to improve performance next month. This can be included, and some would see it as an essential part of the process. The problem I have seen, however, is that this often leads the meeting to focus too much on the past. The review of history is also usually focused on the previous month, and corrective actions usually target the following month. This tends to draw the S&OP down to a short time horizon and turns it into a discussion about the current issues of the day, rather than a longer-term review of where the business is heading over the next 12–24 months. Personally, I would prefer to keep the "last months' review and corrective actions" to an absolute minimum and focus the S&OP meeting on the medium-term future. There are usually other forums, such as daily and monthly management meetings, that provide an opportunity to review current performance and agree on actions to improve performance without bogging the S&OP meeting down in a discussion of the same issues.

There is also a desire (particularly by finance managers) to include a financial forecast in the S&OP process. In theory, this seems like a great idea, but in reality, it can knock the S&OP meeting completely off track. The discussion will inevitably turn to how the business will achieve its sales and profit targets. Debate becomes internally focused, and the true purpose of the S&OP is quickly lost. Instead, the focus of S&OP needs to be firmly on matching demand and supply so we can continue to deliver on time, in full in the future. Therefore, always present the forecast in terms of units of output, not dollars. There will be plenty of other opportunities to discuss the financials in other meetings.

Senior managers are busy people, so it is not a good idea to load them with a huge pile of data and spreadsheets to read as preparation before the meeting. Just highlight the key points and decisions that need to be made in a summary before the meeting. For example, will capital investment be required, do people need to be hired or laid off, or do products or processes need to be outsourced (or insourced)? By providing some data about these issues in advance, you enable the managers to come prepared to discuss them and make decisions in the meeting.

By focusing the S&OP meeting in this way, having a clear agenda, and being well prepared, you then can offer the senior management team a clear benefit—an effective S&OP meeting that will only occupy no more than one hour of their valuable time per week (Table 4.5).

Table 4.5 Inputs and Outputs from S&OP Meeting

Inputs	Outputs
High-level summary of forecast demand by value stream for 12–24 months in the future Summary of capacity model Key assumptions in forecast and capacity models Key risks and opportunities in the forecast period Key changes to people, products, and assets required to meet the expected demand and the rationale behind those	Agreement of forecast, capacity model, and associated assumptions Approval of key actions required to meet forecast demand (or agreement of alternative actions) Agreed on actions to mitigate risks and maximize opportunities identified in forecast period

Overview of S&OP

S&OP is often presented as a complex process reserved for big companies and supply chain experts. In fact, it is a very simple concept that goes to the very heart of your business's ability to deliver on time and in full to your customers: what do we need to deliver, and what steps do we need to take in order to ensure that we can deliver it? Unless your demand and product range are completely stable from month to month and year to year, then you need to consider this question well in advance. Major changes, such as hiring people and purchasing machines, take time, and it is better and far less expensive to plan for these in a structured way than to wait for supply problems or excess capacity to emerge and then try to react in a hurry. Sales and operations planning provides a structured and effective way for your business to communicate about supply and demand. This will make sure that you give yourself the best opportunity to deliver on time and in full every time.

Key Points in Chapter 4

- To achieve reliable on-time, in-full delivery, your business needs to match its medium-term capacity to customer demand.
- For capacity to meet demand, the cycle time achieved by every step in your process has to be less than or equal to takt time.
- To know whether you have enough capacity to meet demand, you can create a simple capacity plan. This can be effectively communicated through a graph of capacity and demand.
- The capacity of your process is limited by the process with the longest cycle time, which is the bottleneck. Provided that the bottleneck process can meet takt time, the remainder of the process will also be able to keep up. Therefore, a capacity plan only needs to regularly compare demand with the bottleneck. However, bottlenecks can sometimes change due to changes in product mix and your process. As a result, it pays to check capacity across your whole process from time to time.
- S&OP is a simple and effective way to ensure that your business will have the resources and capacity to meet expected customer demand.
- S&OP is a monthly cycle that reviews supply and demand. The typical steps in an S&OP process are
  - A demand review where the rolling monthly forecast is reviewed and updated

- A supply review where the capacity and resources needed to meet the expected demand are determined
- An S&OP meeting where senior leaders decide whether to proceed with the changes necessary to meet expected customer demand

Chapter 5

Managing Inventory—If You Do Not Have It, You Cannot Sell It

What You Will Learn in This Chapter

- *The reasons inventory is necessary*
- *The difference between a make-to-stock and make-to-order finished goods strategy*
- *Calculating safety stock and the right level of inventory*
- *Using a pull system to replenish finished goods*
- *Measuring stock-outs and inventory accuracy*
- *Managing make-to-order supply to ensure on-time delivery*

Do You Need Inventory?

In Lean terms, you know that inventory is waste. Your customers are unlikely to pay you one cent more for your product if you hold warehouses of inventory than if you could meet their needs and hold no inventory at all. So why should you hold inventory? Understanding *why* inventory is being held is perhaps the key to deciding how much (if any) inventory to hold.

Let's take a very simple example. Imagine that your customer always purchased one product per day and you knew what that product would be. You would not need inventory. You could just produce or obtain that one product each day, the customer would buy that product, and you would deliver on time every day.

However, what if there was a delay, for example, you ran short of a material, there was a delay in shipping, or a machine broke down in your factory or at your supplier's factory. Alternatively, what if your customer decided to order two products and you only had one? When your customer placed their order, you would not have the product available and you would let them down.

After reflecting on this problem, you might decide that the risk of either your process or supply chain failing to deliver one product or the customer needing more than one product was too great and you could not afford to let the customer down this way. In this case, you would probably decide to have one product ready to sell in advance of the customer order. In other words, you would carry one product in inventory.

Inventory exists because the world is not perfect, the customer does not order the same thing every day, and supply problems do happen (although your Lean management system should be aiming to eliminate them). Holding inventory is your risk mitigation strategy to make sure that you deliver what the customer needs on time and in full every day.

This decision of whether to hold stock is called your finished goods strategy, that is, the strategy you will use to ensure that the goods your customer needs are available to supply on time, in full every time they are ordered. What I have described is a very simple "ex-stock" finished goods strategy. In manufacturing, this is called "make-to-stock." You manufacture or purchase inventory so that when the customer places his or her order, you can pick the products they need off the shelves in your warehouse. If you sell through a distribution or store network, it is likely that your products will be make-to-stock or ex-stock.

For make-to-stock items, successful on-time, in-full delivery requires you to have the right inventory available in the right quantities, always on the shelf of your warehouse, ready meet customer demand.

The Other Finished Goods Strategy: Make-to-Order

There could be another response to our simple scenario. Perhaps our customer is prepared to wait a week for their product. In this case, if our product was delayed or the customer increased their demand, there would not be a problem, provided we could still provide the product within the order lead time that the customer expected (one week). As long as you could supply the product in less than one week, then you would not need to hold inventory. This is called a make-to-order finished goods strategy. In a distribution business, this is often called a "back-to-back" order because the customer's order is matched back-to-back with the order on the supplier that it triggers. Make-to-order strategies are used usually when the product is customized to your customers' individual needs, and especially when the product is a one-off and might never be purchased again. It can also be used for very low-volume products that you do not want to hold in stock and where your customer understands this and is happy to wait for delivery.

*In a make-to-order finished goods strategy, inventory made in advance for specific customer orders should be the **only** finished goods inventory you carry (and even this should be minimized).*

Make-to-order products are usually customized or one-off products made for a specific customer order. If you make inventory when the customer has not placed an order (perhaps anticipating a future order), you run a very high risk that the customer will not place that anticipated order and your inventory will become obsolete.

Managing Your Finished Goods Strategy

It is important to stick to the "rules" of your finished goods strategy. Make-to-stock items should always be in stock ready to sell, and make-to-order items should only be in in stock if they are waiting for shipment to fulfill a specific customer order. I routinely find businesses offering ex-stock delivery when in fact much of their product range is not held in stock on the shelf. When the customer orders these products, they will be let down and disappointed. I also find warehouses full of make-to-order products made for a specific customer need because the company has taken a "bet" that the customer will place another order for the same product. Too often, this turns out to be a losing bet and the stock becomes obsolete.

It is possible that your business will have a combination of make-to-stock and make-to-order products, depending on the individual demand characteristics of your product range. We will talk more about make-to-order supply at the end of this chapter.

How Much Inventory Do You Need of Make-to-Stock Items?

There are five factors affecting the amount of inventory you need:

1. Replenishment lead time: The lead time it takes you to replenish the inventory from when you trigger replenishment until the replacement stock is on the shelf. This could be your internal manufacturing lead time, if you are a manufacturer; your replenishment lead time from your supplier; or a combination of both.
2. Replenishment interval: The frequency in which you replenish the inventory.
3. Replenishment quantity: The quantity that you order each time you replenish.
4. The amount of variability in units of customer demand measured by the standard deviation of customer demand (σ_D).
5. The amount of variability in days of supply lead time measured by the standard deviation of lead time (σ_{LT}).

Figure 5.1 shows a typical replenishment cycle for inventory. As you can see, inventory levels drop until they reach a preset level called the minimum stock or reorder point. At this point, a new order for a preset replenishment quantity is triggered. In the case of Figure 5.1, the replenishment quantity ordered is 300 units and the reorder point has been calculated as 130 units. Inventory will then fall below the reorder point until the replacement inventory arrives; however, the quantity of safety stock is sufficient to ensure that inventory does not run out completely during the replenishment period. From Figure 5.1, you can see that the replenishment interval varies between two and four days, depending on the level of customer demand. The average replenishment interval is simply the replenishment quantity divided by the average daily demand.

To set the reorder point or minimum stock level, we have to consider how much inventory will be used over the replenishment lead time. This is simply the average daily usage times the replenishment lead time. However, customer demand varies from day to day and week to week, and our replenishment lead time may also sometimes vary. Therefore, we need an additional amount of stock over and above the average usage to allow for this variation. We call this additional stock safety stock. The equation below summarizes how you calculate the reorder point or minimum stock level.

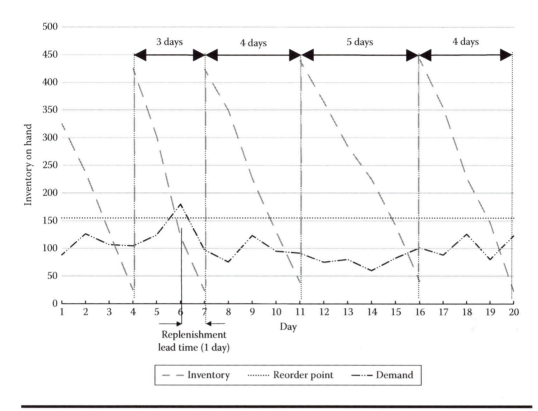

Figure 5.1 **Graph showing daily inventory levels in a fixed-quantity, variable-interval replenishment cycle.**

Reorder point $=$ (Replenishment lead time $\times$ Average daily sales) $+$ Safety stock

Calculating Safety Stock

One of the most important decisions you will need to make is how much safety stock to hold. Get it wrong and your business will be saddled with excess stock or else you will find yourself constantly running out of stock and letting customers down. There are PhDs written on the subject of calculating safety stock. However, from my experience, I am not convinced that the complex approaches deliver a better result than the simple methods. The important things to remember are

■ Safety stock is not a constant. It should regularly be reviewed and adjusted to reflect changes in customer demand and your supply chain. Reviewing safety stock should probably occur at least every quarter as part of the supply review process in your sales and operations planning (S&OP) cycle (see Chapter 4 for more on S&OP).

■ Safety stock depends on the individual supply chain characteristics of the individual value stream. Many companies will shortcut the safety stock process by just applying a blanket figure, for example, one month's safety stock for everything. You can be sure that this will be too much safety stock for half the product you supply and not enough for the other half. The level of safety stock is a function of the individual demand for that product. Therefore, it needs to be calculated individually for each product. You may also choose to vary safety stock depending on the importance of the product, so that you tolerate a lower risk of shortages for high-value, high-margin items, but a higher risk for less important products.

I am not a supporter of the "dynamic safety stock" systems built into some software. This functionality constantly adjusts safety stock based on changes in the forecast. In my experience, dynamic safety stock tends to inject more instability into the supply chain by constantly changing the point at which stock is triggered. As a result, the effects of forecast inaccuracy are amplified.

One of the key assumptions behind calculating safety stock is that the level of inventory and the reliability of service you can offer is a trade-off. If you want to maintain every product in stock, 100% of the time, and always achieve 100% on-time, in-full delivery, you will find yourself holding a lot of inventory. Likewise, if you decide to cut inventory, your service levels will decline accordingly. Therefore, to calculate safety stock, you need to decide the level of on-time, in-full delivery you are targeting.

Some simple formulas using some basic statistics can be used to calculate safety stock.* The typical measure of how much a parameter such as demand or lead time varies from its average value is called standard deviation. To calculate safety stock, we need to calculate the standard deviation of demand over replenishment lead time (σ_D). If your replenishment lead time is longer than your replenishment interval and the lead time varies (such as if you are importing goods), then you also need to look at your historical orders and calculate the standard deviation of lead time (σ_{LT}) in days. We then use a very handy statistical figure known as the Z score or standard score. The Z score tells us what multiple of standard deviation we will need to apply in order to have confidence that demand will not exceed that

---

* King, P. L. Crack the code—Understanding safety stock and mastering its equations. *APICS Magazine*, July/August 2011.

Table 5.1   Relationship between *Z* Score and Stock Availability

Target Stock Availability (%)	Z Score
84	1.0
90	1.28
95	1.65
97	1.88
98	2.05
99	2.33
99.5	3.09

level. The higher the *Z* score, the higher our confidence that demand will not exceed our safety stock and that we will therefore not run out of stock. The *Z* score allows us to target a level of stock availability for each item (Table 5.1).

If your replenishment lead time is less than your replenishment interval, then safety stock is simply

$$\text{Safety stock} = Z \times \sigma_D$$

If the replenishment lead time exceeds the replenishment interval, then the formula becomes slightly more complex, as you need to calculate your standard deviation of demand, σ_D, for the replenishment interval and then multiply by the square root of the ratio of your replenishment lead time, *LT*, and your replenishment interval, *I*. The formula then becomes

$$\text{Safety stock} = Z \times \sigma_D \times \sqrt{\frac{LT}{I}}$$

With long lead times, you may also need to consider the variation in your replenishment lead time as measured by σ_{LT}. In this case, the formula becomes

$$\text{Safety stock} = Z \times \sqrt{((\frac{LT}{I} \times \sigma_D^2) + (\sigma_{LT} \times D_{AVG})^2)}$$

where D_{AVG} equals the average demand over the replenishment interval (*I*).

Using standard deviation to calculate safety stock has some limitations. If there is a lot of seasonality or strong upward or downward trends, this will show up as extra variation and will tend to bias the safety stock upward compared with where it needs to be. You can eliminate seasonality by doing separate safety stock calculations for the busy months and the quiet months (remember, as I said above, safety stock levels need to be regularly reviewed). It is good to apply a commonsense test to your safety stock. If you do the statistical calculation and find it is recommending stock levels that are far above what you have ever sold, then this approach may not be right for you. Perhaps you do not have enough historical data for the product concerned, or "special causes," such as promotions, are showing up as "variation." You might want to simply take these special causes out of the safety stock calculation. You might also find that customer demand is regularly exceeding the calculated safety stock. In this case, a closer examination of the demand is required to see patterns. Is there one-off demand occurring, or are activities such as price increases causing demand spikes? Another problem can be that for low-volume items that are sold infrequently, the calculated weekly usage and safety stock may end up being less than the typical quantity your customer purchases. For these items, you may need to manually adjust safety stock based on the quantity your customer is likely to purchase or, even better, convince the customer to allow a lead time on supply and treat them as make-to-order products. I am sure you can see that effective communication through your S&OP process is essential for understanding your demand and making the right decisions on safety stock.

Avoiding the Knee-Jerk Response to a Shortage

In many businesses, the occurrence of a stock shortage will cause a "knee-jerk" reflexive response—"increase the safety stock!" Sometimes, these reactive stock increases stay in place for years after the incident that triggered them. In reality, an inventory shortage can be caused by any number of things, including a one-off spike in customer demand, an unexpected interruption in supply, a quality issue, or a poorly planned promotion. In Lean thinking, we aim to "solve problems using scientific method," as characterized by the plan–do–check–act problem-solving method. This should also be applied to shortages. The steps are

- Identify the root cause of the problem. This may require discussion with suppliers or your customer to understand the reasons for any supply or demand fluctuation. Try to work out whether the shortage was a result of normal demand or supply variation (a common cause) or a one-off event (a special cause).

■ Agree on a corrective action. If the shortage occurred as a result of normal supply or demand variation, then perhaps it is worth looking at your safety stock formula and making adjustments. However, if the problem is a one-off special cause, then you need to understand the reasons for that event and the likely frequency of those events (will it ever happen again?), and agree on corrective actions to prevent future shortages. This may involve strategies other than additional inventory, such as improving communication with the customer, sourcing a backup supplier, or making improvements to the reliability of your process.

■ Check the corrective action. Monitor the inventory of the product over the following weeks and months. Are there further shortages, or do you find now that you typically have too much stock? Further adjustment might be necessary to get the level of safety stock and the supply chain for this product right.

■ Once you are satisfied that the improvements are preventing future shortages (or overstocking), then lock this in by adjusting your safety stock settings or the underlying calculation and recording the assumptions behind that change. In the case of supply chain changes, you might want to update service level agreements with suppliers or the agenda and procedures for your S&OP process. Also think about other products. Could they be affected by the same problem, and therefore should the learnings from the problem with one product be applied to others?

This sounds like a lot of work, and it is. Perhaps it seems easier when you have a shortage to just increase the safety stock and move on. However, by taking this shortcut, you are failing to address the underlying problem and may be saddling your business with unnecessary excess stock. Most importantly, if the level of safety stock is *not* the root cause of the shortage (and in most cases it isn't), then you can expect to have more shortages of that part even if you have increased the safety stock.

Types of Pull Replenishment

In Chapter 2, I described the difference between push and pull approaches to replenishment. In writing this chapter, I have assumed that you will be using the pull method to replenish your finished goods. The reasons for this are hopefully clear in the explanations I have provided in Chapter 3 about the limitations of replenishing based on forecasts. Chapter 4 has also explained how you can account for future variation in demand using a sales and operations process.

In a Lean supply chain, we use pull replenishment because we are more likely to get lower inventory and avoid shortages by replenishing off actual usage rather than relying on forecasts that are likely to be inaccurate. So how would the pull system actually work in practice? The replenishment models described in this chapter are both based on pull principles, but there are different types of pull systems.

The reorder point replenishment that I have shown in Figure 5.1 is called *fixed-quantity, variable-interval* replenishment because the time between one order and the next will vary depending on customer demand, but the replenishment quantity is fixed. A critical requirement of this model of replenishment is that the replenishment quantity must exceed the reorder point. Otherwise, when the replacement stock arrives, stock levels will not be replenished back up to the reorder point, further replenishment will not be triggered, and you will eventually run out. As a result, this simple replenishment model can lead to high levels of inventory for long-lead-time items.

An alternative approach to replenishment is *variable-quantity, fixed-interval* replenishment. This is shown in Figure 5.2. In this model of replenishment, inventory is replenished at a constant interval (in the Figure 5.2, this is every five days), but the quantity ordered varied. The amount to order is calculated from subtracting the stock on hand at the time the order is placed from the target stock where the target stock is calculated as

$$\text{Target stock} = (\text{Average daily sales} \times \text{Replenishment interval}) + \text{Safety stock}$$

And the quantity to order is calculated as

$$\text{Order quantity} = \text{Target stock} - \text{Stock on hand}$$

Using a fixed-interval, variable-quantity replenishment cycle has advantages when your factory or your supplier is able to provide a variable quantity to meet your demand. The regular ordering pattern can often make planning simpler and more predictable. Your supplier or factory expects your order at the same time every day, week, or month and can plan their process to match your order cycle. We highly recommend using this

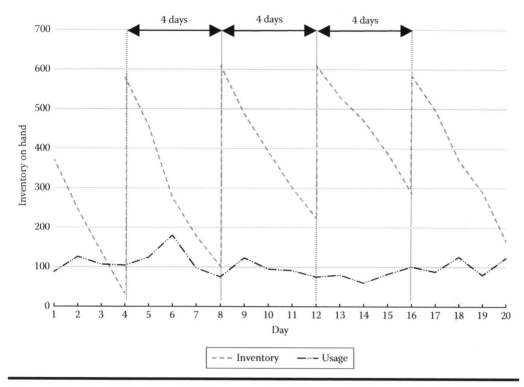

Figure 5.2   Graph showing daily inventory levels in a variable-quantity, fixed-interval replenishment cycle.

approach when sourcing materials through international supply chains, as we discuss in Chapter 8.

These replenishment methods are typically managed through system reports in an enterprise resource planning (ERP) system or in a spreadsheet. "Min-max" replenishment functionality is usually a standard capability within most ERP systems. The challenge with replenishing off system stock rather than physical stock is that the inventory in the system must be accurate; otherwise, you will be continually ordering the wrong things at the wrong time. Therefore, in many cases a replenishment system based on physical stock can be more accurate and effective.

Kanban Cards

The most recognizable form of physical pull replenishment is the Kanban card. This is a pre-prepared card (usually kept inside a protective plastic sleeve) that represents one container or pack of inventory. Figure 5.3 shows an example of a Kanban card. When that inventory is sold or consumed,

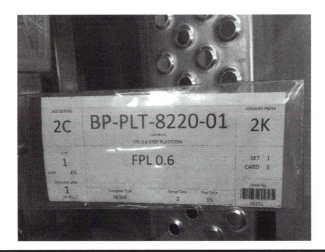

Figure 5.3   Example of a Kanban card used to trigger replenishment of finished goods.

the card is detached from the container and returned to production control to trigger manufacturing of replacement stock, or is sent to purchasing, who will purchase the replacement stock. Once the replacement stock arrives, the cards are attached to the new containers and the cycle starts over again. Figure 5.4 shows the use of Kanban cards to replenish ladders. When a ladder is sold, the card is removed and returned to the load leveling box shown in Figure 5.5 to trigger replenishment.*

The amount of stock maintained in inventory for each product is determined by the number of Kanban cards in circulation for that product. This is calculated in a way similar to that of the safety stock calculations using the formula below:

Number of Kanban cards in circulation for each part =

$$\frac{(\text{Average daily demand} \times \text{Replenishment lead time}) + \text{Safety stock}}{\text{Quantity per container}}$$

As discussed above, when the replenishment lead time is long, min-max or reorder point replenishment can lead to high levels of inventory. In fact, the "reorder point" model of replenishment is really like a Kanban system where you only have two cards. It is also called a "two-bin system." If you allow multiple cards, then a Kanban system allows you to have multiple orders in process for standard quantities, meaning that for long-lead-time

---

* An explanation of load leveling boxes is provided in Chapter 6.

Figure 5.4   Kanban cards attached to finished ladders.

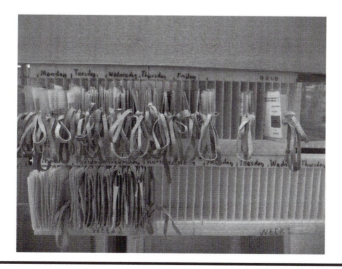

Figure 5.5   Load leveling box. When the ladder in Figure 5.4 is sold, the Kanban card is detached and returned to this box to trigger replenishment.

items, you will receive regular smaller deliveries of products during the replenishment lead time rather than having to wait for one large delivery.

For an excellent description of the various types of Kanban, including formulas to use, I recommend you look at *Creating Level Pull* by Art Smalley.* This book will also help you understand some of the concepts I will introduce in Chapter 6.

Other Forms of Pull Systems

In many cases, it is simply not practical to attach a Kanban card to every single container of finished goods in a warehouse. In this case, a range of other mechanisms might be used to trigger replenishment.

If the product range is simple, then visual replenishment might be used. In this case, an area on the floor or a range of pallet racking locations are allocated for each part number. In a fixed-interval replenishment model, someone will then be assigned the job to regularly count the number of empty stock locations for each part, and this will then form the order for that part. Figure 5.6 shows an example of a pull system using color-coded "Kanban squares."

Figure 5.6 Example of color-coded Kanban squares. When the bins are emptied and the yellow area on the floor exposed, this triggers replenishment. Exposure of a red area highlights potential shortages and triggers expedited replenishment.

* Smalley, A. 2004. *Creating Level Pull: A Lean Production System Improvement Guide for Production-Control, Operations and Engineering Professionals.* Brookline, MA: Lean Enterprise Institute.

Virtual Kanban

When supply chains are widely dispersed or even international, it becomes impractical to transfer physical Kanban cards from location to location. In this case, a "virtual Kanban" system can be effective. An off-line spreadsheet records each Kanban quantity even though there is not a physical Kanban in use. Like other system-based solutions, it requires accurate reconciliation between physical and system inventory.

This worked very effectively at a paint factory I worked with several years ago. The Kanban "trigger" was the transfer of a full pallet of product from a bulk location in the racks to a picking location. The Kanban quantity was one pallet of products. For each product, a designated number of Kanbans were maintained in the system, whether they were in stock, waiting in queue for replenishment, or actually in the process of being manufactured.

Stock-Outs: A Leading Indicator of On-Time, In-Full Performance

To ensure that you can deliver to your customer on time and in full, you need to ensure that you always have inventory on the shelf of your ex-stock items. An effective measure of this is the number of stock-outs. A stock-out is a stocked line where there is currently nil stock. It is simply measured as the ratio of the number of products that are currently in stock to the total number of items that should be in stock. Clearly, if products are not in stock, this will lead directly to a delivery in-full, on-time (DIFOT) "miss" when these products are ordered. If your replenishment system is operating correctly, then you should always have stock of all your ex-stock inventory items.

$$\text{Stock} - \text{outs} = \frac{\text{Number of line items with zero stock}}{\text{Total number of ex-stock line items}} \times \frac{100\%}{1}$$

To make it even simpler, I often suggest to companies that they simply target keeping stock-outs below a maximum number of line items. This often means more to frontline warehouse staff than percentages. For example, you may have a target of no more than 10 ex-stock items out of stock at any time.

You may also choose to refine the measure further by setting separate targets for your highest-volume items. For example, you may target no more than 10 stock-outs in total with no more than 2 stock-outs of high-volume "Class A" items.

Inventory Record Accuracy

If you are using an electronic system such as an ERP system to trigger stock replenishment, then it is vital that the inventory levels recorded in your system match the actual levels on the shelf to a high degree of accuracy. Otherwise, when you run reports to trigger replenishment, you will be triggering either too soon or too late. Inventory record accuracy is the ratio of the number of products where the stock on the system matches the stock on the shelf. Often, a tolerance will be allowed for a small amount of stock shrinkage, particularly for products and materials stored in bulk. Therefore, provided the stock on the shelf is within ±5% of the quantity on the system, the stock is considered to be accurate. A further level of accuracy is to measure location accuracy. This is the ratio of the number of stock locations in the warehouse where the correct item is stored in the correct quantity to the total number of active locations.

The most effective way to measure inventory record accuracy is through cycle counts. Cycle counts involve dividing the warehouse into a number of zones and then setting a schedule to count these zones progressively over a period of time (usually every 6–12 weeks, depending on the size of the warehouse). The warehouse team set a number of locations to count per day and can measure inventory record accuracy for the locations counted each day.

Managing Make-to-Order Supply to Achieve On-Time, In-Full Delivery

For make-to-order supply, the first thing you need to determine is the order fulfillment lead time you need to achieve. Put simply, the correct order fulfillment lead time is the lead time your customer expects. Competitive advantage can be gained by offering a shorter lead time than your competitors—as long as you can sustain this. Problems occur when the customer's expectation of lead time is shorter than the order fulfillment lead time your business can deliver. Therefore, for make-to-order products, being able to consistently supply products in an order fulfillment lead time that is equal to or less than the customer's expectation is critical if you are to deliver on time and in full.

A door manufacturer we worked with had an agreement to supply custom-made doors to a key customer within four days of order. When we completed a value stream map of their process, we found that the actual order lead time was around 17 days. Much energy was expended expediting orders for doors to ensure that the "urgent" ones were delivered on time, and renegotiating delivery dates on the less urgent ones. This led to low productivity, poor on-time delivery, and considerable stress and frustration all round. We worked with the customer to design a new future state for the business where the order fulfillment lead time for all doors was less than three days. This meant that the four-day lead time could comfortably be met.

For make-to-order products, customer demand will also vary. If your order fulfillment lead time exactly equals the lead time the customer expects, any short-term increase in customer demand will cause you to let the customer down. Therefore, your order fulfillment lead time needs to be significantly less (usually 30%–50% less) than the lead time expected by the customer. This usually takes the form of a small backlog of orders waiting to be released to production. If you are a distributor, you will probably maintain this backlog as a list of open orders on your supplier. This backlog is necessary to buffer out variation in customer demand. If demand goes up, then the backlog increases, but because your customer is expecting a longer lead time than you can actually achieve, you can still supply the goods within the customer's expected lead time. When demand drops, then you have the opportunity to catch up and reduce the backlog.

Beyond lead time buffers, it can be helpful if your factory (or supplier) has some flexibility in working hours. Usually, this means working overtime on weekends or extending shifts to handle peak demand or even moving to a "short week" to handle low demand. This is why 24-hour, 7-day production is not really suited for make-to-order production. If you are already working 24/7, you cannot extend your working hours further.

Another option might be to maintain spare production capacity, such as extra production lines that you can switch on in peak periods. This is a capital-intensive solution, so it is usually only used in highly seasonal businesses.

Several years ago, we worked with a rowing boat builder. Rowing is highly seasonal, as the peak sales period is the lead-up to summer (when people go rowing) and around major regattas. This company prided themselves on making a customized product, but unfortunately, their backlog of boats on order had blown out to six months. We agreed on a target customer order lead time with them of six weeks from order to delivery to deliver a customized boat. To achieve this, all three strategies outlined above were employed.

■ *The production process was designed to deliver an order fulfillment lead time of three weeks, giving three weeks lead time buffer to manage the backlog.*
■ *Short-term demand spikes could be managed by working on Saturday.*
■ *In peak season, a second production line was started, doubling production for three or four months.*

Summary

Inventory management is a huge subject and the focus of many books and much research. It is therefore important to remember the basics:

■ Inventory exists because customers do not order the same quantity every day. Demand is variable. Therefore, inventory needs to be held to allow for these variations.
■ Your finished goods strategy is the business rule you set for each product or group of products that determines the circumstances under which finished goods stock will be held. There are two main finished goods strategies—make-to-stock (or ex-stock) or make-to-order.
■ If your supplier expects you to deliver in a lead time that is less than the lead time you require to replenish your inventory, then you require inventory and need to apply a make-to-stock approach. If not, you can operate a make-to-order strategy where you only manufacture or purchase products for the customer *after* they place their order and not carry stock of those goods.
■ The inventory you need to hold in a make-to-stock finished goods strategy typically needs to allow for the average usage of that product plus an allowance for variation in your supply chain and in the customer's demand. We call this allowance safety stock. Safety stock can be calculated using simple statistical formulas that allow for the level of variation in your supply and demand.
■ You need to apply a "commonsense test" to calculated safety stock to allow for known exceptions, such as seasonal variations, promotions, or other significant one-off changes to demand.

- Pull systems give better outcomes for replenishment of stock in terms of inventory levels and frequency of shortages because they do not rely on inaccurate forecasts. There are several different types of pull systems, and the right one for you will depend on the particular characteristics of your product range and your supply chain.

- Replenishment based on inventory levels recorded in a computer system (rather than physical inventory) relies on the maintenance of high levels of inventory record accuracy if you are to avoid shortages. If you cannot maintain this level of inventory accuracy, it can be more effective to replenish off physical inventory movements using a pull system.

- To keep track of your inventory management performance, it is a good idea to measure the number of stocked items that are out of stock at any time. This is a good predictor of your on-time delivery performance, because in a make-to-stock environment, if you do not have it in stock, you cannot sell it.

- In a make-to-order finished goods strategy, your lead time needs to match your customers' and the market's expectation. In a make-to-order environment, you cannot hold finished goods inventory to buffer out variation in customer demand. Therefore, it is important that your internal process lead time be significantly below the lead time that you promise to customers in order to provide this buffer.

Chapter 6

What Should We Make Next? The Keys to Production Scheduling

What You Will Learn in This Chapter

- *Why forecast-based production scheduling usually leads to expediting, high levels of inventory, and poor delivery performance*
- *The concept of pacemaker—why you only plan at one point and how to decide where that point is located in your process*
- *Using a load leveling box to control the rate of release of work to production*
- *Selecting the pitch interval for your process—deciding how much work to release to production and how often to release it*
- *How to decide the sequence of production and level out your product mix using repetitive flexible supply and product wheels*

This chapter is focused on production planning. If you are in a distribution business, you may want to skip to Chapter 7. Alternatively, it may be useful to learn about production planning to better understand what might be going wrong at your key suppliers.

What to Do Next: The Planning Question

In Chapter 4, we established a sales and operations plan. This provides a high-level view of your supply and demand and will enable you to plan your capacity and long-range requirements for materials. But how do you decide what you should make next week or the next day? In fact, how do you decide what you will make *next* after the current job finishes? This is crucial, because you have to decide what to make *before* your customer needs it, and therefore if you make the wrong decision, you are likely to make the wrong product at the wrong time, have the wrong inventory, and let your customer down. So how *do* you decide what to make next?

What I have seen over the years is that, in many businesses, the process of production scheduling is a little like watching a duck sailing across a pond. On the surface, all appears calm and smooth. The enterprise resource planning (ERP) system runs a planning program called material requirements planning (MRP*) every night. MRP creates production requirements for every work cell based on the forecast. Perhaps advanced planning and optimization software even applies finite scheduling to optimize capacity and decide the ideal sequence for production. Everything just glides along to the accompaniment of the quiet hum of powerful computers. That is usually the theory promoted by the supply chain manager and the information technology (IT) manager as they present their successful implementation of the most advanced planning software. However, the *reality* in *every* company I have seen is that beneath this calm surface, somewhere deep in the organization, is a group of people who are like the legs of the duck, paddling furiously underwater to keep the "duck" on track. These people are schedulers, buyers, and production managers, who often spend their days adjusting schedules, expediting jobs and materials, and moving labor around to make sure that customers get what they need when they need it in the right quantity. In Chapter 3, I have explored the reasons for all this furious activity.

MRP planning is built on a forecast, and the forecast is inevitably wrong.

Therefore, the MRP system will more often than not plan the wrong production at the wrong time, and the advanced planning and optimization software will then schedule the wrong products in the right sequence. Add to that the fact that most companies struggle to keep the data in their ERP system accurate. If parameters such as inventory levels, batch sizes, and lead times are not completely accurate, the MRP will give you the wrong answer

---

* See Chapter 10 for a more detailed overview of the functions of an ERP system, including MRP.

even if the forecast is perfectly accurate (which it isn't). You can quickly see why the team has to paddle so hard under the water!

So, if the forecast-driven planning model doesn't work, what does? The answer is surprisingly simple to understand, but takes a lot of discipline to implement. In this chapter, we discuss how to create a simple and effective process for production planning and scheduling.

Typical Production Planning Scenario

When we complete a current state map at a new customer, what we usually see looks like Figure 6.1. This example shows the flow of production for a manufacturer of steel doors. Like many metal manufacturing processes, it features a number of process steps. The process started with the manufacture of door components. An automated, computer numerically controlled (CNC) turret punch cut out blank components that were then folded and welded together on CNC brake presses and robotic welding machines. These welded components were then fed into a batch powder coating process. The painted parts were then supplied to manual assembly, and finally, completed doors were transferred to another building for packaging. A typical centralized planning and scheduling process was used. Orders were entered into a simple ERP system. This produced a report showing the expected due dates of these orders. Production schedules were then produced on Microsoft Excel for each department with an aim of achieving the expected order delivery dates. Conflicts then occurred because the supervisor of the sheet metal area would aim to maximize his efficiency by grouping orders in terms of door size and style in order to reduce the number of tool changes on the brake presses and welding robots. However, the powder coating supervisor would want to group orders according to color. As a result, hundreds of components would accumulate in the welding area, waiting for long runs of each size to be completed. Dozens more door frames would queue up waiting for sufficient frames of one color to be accumulated to justify changing color on the powder coating line. Painted doors were then assembled based on which were the most urgent orders. When all these work-in-progress buffers were considered, average lead times were over 17 days. The agreed customer order lead time was only four days, so to provide the appearance of on-time delivery, the factory supervisor spent his day expediting urgent orders to meet customer needs. Of course, all that was achieved was that the most urgent orders were delivered within the four-day expected

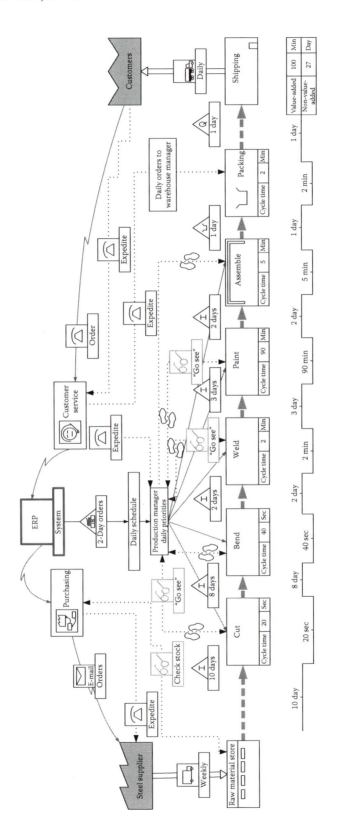

Figure 6.1 Current state map for push production of doors.

lead time, while the remainder often ended up taking much longer than the average 17 days. As well, the expediting meant that the careful plans of the sheet metal and powder coating supervisors to achieve long "efficient" production runs were constantly thwarted by the need to break into runs to complete urgent orders. As you can imagine, the production manager was an incredibly busy and highly stressed individual.

This situation is extremely common in manufacturing processes. Often, production managers and production planners will proudly proclaim their planning rules, when closer observation shows that these rules are broken on a daily, if not hourly, basis in what is usually a vain effort to achieve on-time delivery. Production plans are "honored in the breach."

This approach is called push production, where each step of the production process attempts to manufacture what it expects that the next step will need in the future. I liken this approach to an orchestra conductor separating the different parts of the score and providing it to the leaders of each of the sections of the orchestra—strings, brass, woodwind, and percussion. The leaders of each section would then be free to play their individual scores to the best of their ability, based on the plan, without the overall guidance of the conductor. You can imagine what would happen. Very quickly, the different orchestra sections would get out of time and the noise would be terrible. Instead, as we all know, the conductor conducts the whole orchestra, ensuring that all the sections play together in time and produce beautiful music.

Managing Production Flow with a Pacemaker

In a Lean production environment, the first step to overcoming these problems is choosing one point in the value stream where you will schedule production. This point is called the pacemaker process. The pacemaker process is the conductor of your value stream. It sets the beat of production and ensures that everyone acts in harmony.

Production is released at the pacemaker process, and so the sequence of what is going to be made is set there. Product must always "flow" downstream of the pacemaker, meaning that downstream processes must always follow the sequence of production set by the pacemaker. Production orders flow one at a time in "one-piece flow" or a first-in, first-out (FIFO) sequence from one downstream process to the next. Upstream of the pacemaker, parts and subassemblies are "pulled" to the pacemaker to replenish materials that have been consumed by the pacemaker. The upstream processes do not produce anything unless it has been pulled by the pacemaker. This pull signal is often communicated by a Kanban card.

This is best illustrated by returning to our door manufacturing example. Figure 6.2 shows the future state map we developed from the current state value stream map shown in Figure 6.1. In the future state, the pacemaker process is powder coating. Therefore, orders are released to powder coating. This triggers painting of door jambs. Downstream of powder coating, the door jams flow in a FIFO sequence to assembly with a door frame and door skin. The assembled doors then flow in one-piece flow through assembly and packaging, which have now been combined into a single cell. Upstream of powder coating, unpainted door jambs are pulled through cutting, folding, and welding using a Kanban system.

There is no need to have separate production plans for punching, folding, welding, or assembly. For each of these processes, the sequence of production is set by the sequence of orders arriving at the work cell. The sequence of production is only set at the powder coating cell.

Finding the Correct Unit of Measure and Pitch Interval

In the door factory, the takt time was around 180 seconds. It is difficult to track production every 180 seconds, and keeping track of the progress of every single door would be difficult. Therefore, it is necessary to decide on the frequency at which work is released at the pacemaker. This is called the pitch. In this case, the pitch was chosen to be 36 minutes. This meant that 12 doors were released to the pacemaker at powder coating every 36 minutes. Purpose-built door trolleys were made to transport exactly 12 doors (Figure 6.3) from process to process. Therefore, once the 12 frames were painted, they were kept together on these trolleys right through production. These trolleys also provided a very simple visual indicator of work in progress and made the doors easy to move from process to process.

Using a Load Leveling Box

Controlling the work at the pacemaker is usually done using a very simple tool called a load leveling box (also known as a *Heijunka* box from the Japanese term for leveling). Figure 6.4 is a very good example of a load

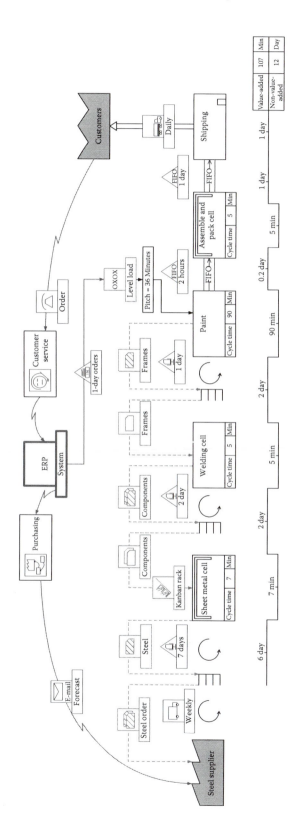

Figure 6.2   Future state map for doors showing how the pacemaker process controls production.

Figure 6.3   Operator stacking doors on a kit trolley.

leveling box. You can see in this case that each slot represents a pitch interval of 20 minutes. The cards in each slot (Kanban cards) are work orders for a set amount of work. The vertical bar is a useful innovation to track the progress of the day. You can see in Figure 6.4 that this photo was taken at 2:20 p.m., and that the cards to the left of this bar are overdue to be pulled out and sent to the line to be produced. In this way, the load leveling box controls the rate of production, sets the sequence of production, and provides a visual indicator every 20 minutes of whether the plant is ahead or behind schedule.

How Long Should the Pitch Interval Be?

There are a number of factors to consider when choosing your pitch interval. If the pitch is too short, then you will find it difficult to keep up with scheduling and a lot of transactional work will be generated. A short pitch interval can also mean that there is no time to take corrective action to keep production on track. On the other hand, if the pitch is too long, production can be a long way off track before a problem is noticed. This makes it much harder to catch up before the end of the shift. For example, if you chose a pitch interval of two hours, production could be two hours behind schedule before anyone noticed and took action. Clearly, it is much harder to catch up two hours of lost production than it is 20 minutes.

Often, there is a logical means of determining pitch interval. Packaging can determine the logical pitch. For example, at a manufacturer of electronic

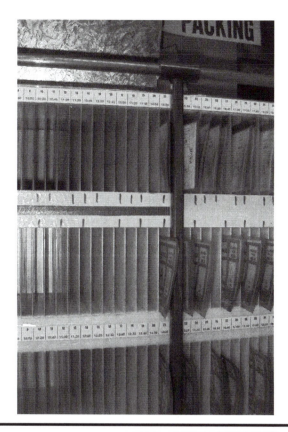

Figure 6.4   Example of a load leveling box with a 20-minute pitch interval.

smoke detectors, we determined the takt time to be six seconds. However, products were packed into cartons of 60. Customers never purchased less than a carton. Therefore, we agreed on a pitch of four cartons, or 24 minutes. It might have been possible to have a shorter pitch, perhaps two cartons and 12 minutes. However, when first implementing level production, it is wise to choose a slightly longer pitch, as this is easier to manage at the start.

In jobbing shops, such as printing, joinery, machining, or sheet metal, or batch processes, such as food, coatings, or chemicals, working out the pitch becomes even more complex. This is because you are trying to manage the flow of completely different products through your operation. In this kind of process, much of the effort and activity is involved in setting up the batch or job. The actual product run can be quite short. Therefore, the determinant of pitch can be the number of batches or jobs. For example, a sheet metal shop produced an average of 170 jobs per month. This translated to eight jobs per day, or one per hour. The pitch interval could then be one hour. Jobs will vary greatly in size, so aim to set your pitch around the "average" size job (which in this case involved around 8–10 hours of labor). If you have small jobs, you might choose to release two at a time, whereas larger jobs might be broken up into parts and released progressively over several pitch intervals. It is not necessary to ensure that every job is exactly the same size provided you "level the product mix" by releasing a mixture of big jobs and small jobs, rather than releasing all the big jobs together on one day and all the small jobs together the next day. I will discuss how to level the mix later in this chapter. By reducing the batch or job size, you can reduce the pitch interval and also improve the flexibility of your process. This avoids tying up key machines or processes for long periods on a single product.

Overview of Pacemakers and Pitch

Much of the complexity of planning comes from the efforts made to plan every single point in a process. Because processes run at different rates and have different constraints and often different and contradictory metrics, this can lead production plans into conflict. Therefore, efforts to optimize each individual point in the production process can badly suboptimize the overall process. Allowing each process to "beat to a different drum" requires large inventory buffers between processes and leads to long lead times (like in the steel doors case study). In addition, the "push" scheduling model, where each process is scheduled separately to meet a forecast, is highly dependent on the accuracy of the forecast and on each individual process performing to plan. When this does not occur, the process quickly breaks down and expediting becomes the order of the day. This then compounds the problems as informal "urgent job lists" and off-line discussions override the formal planning process in a desperate and vain effort to meet customer deadlines.

The recognition that you should only plan at one point in your process is the first step to simple and effective production planning. The need to develop complex plans for every process is immediately removed. Just one plan is needed for each value stream, and that plan simply lists the sequence in which jobs will be started. Since we flow downstream of the pacemaker, the sequence in which jobs are started is also the sequence in which they are finished, rather than having different planning rules and a different sequence at each process. Work in progress in a Lean production system is strictly controlled, and therefore lead time is much more predictable and generally shorter.

Releasing production at a single pacemaker process and leveling the rate of release at a pitch interval greatly simplifies the scheduling of production. For many processes, it does not matter which sequence the orders are released in. In these cases, jobs can just be loaded into the load leveling box in the order in which they are received, or perhaps in the order of customer due date.

However, for some processes, simply releasing orders at the pacemaker according to customer due date or the sequence in which orders are received can lead to a loss of efficiency. Often, there are logical sequences of production that need to be followed in order to reduce unnecessary changeover time.

Deciding What Product to Make Next at the Pacemaker

In many production processes, there is a logical sequence in which orders can be processed. For example, for colored products such as paint or extruded plastics, it is preferable for light colors to be run before dark colors, as the dark colors can often cover up any residue of the light colors left in the process machinery. In many fast-moving consumer goods processes, it is common for processes to be scheduled so that all the products of a given pack size are run first before a complex pack size change is made. In printing, jobs are often grouped by print design, colors, and then die form.

It is common for companies to go to great lengths to develop the "optimum" manufacturing sequence in an attempt to minimize changeover time and maximize output. The inflexibility of these scheduling rules often cannot be sustained, leading to excessive inventory, missed deliveries, and the "ideal sequence" being broken more often than it is followed.

So how can you create efficient production with a stable production schedule while coping with constantly changing customer needs?

Understanding Your Product Mix and Building the Product Cycle

The first point to building a stable production scheduling system is to understand your product mix. To do this, we use a tool called the "Glenday sieve," developed by Ian Glenday and described in detail in his books *Breaking*

Table 6.1   Format of Product Table

Product Ranking	Product Code	Product Description	Annual Sales (volume or value)	Cumulative Sales	% Cumulative Sales

through to Flow* and *Lean RFS.†* Make up a spreadsheet of all your products and rank them from the highest sales volume (in dollars or units—whichever makes the most sense) to lowest. The column titles will look like shown in Table 6.1.

Glenday then suggests you look down the % Cumulative Sales column. In almost every case, you see a clear pattern where a small percentage of the products represent a large percentage of the business's revenue. Typical results might look like shown in Table 6.2.

The different categories of products then require a different approach to scheduling:

■ "Green" products are high-volume items that can be arranged into a fixed logical production cycle and run frequently (usually daily, but at most weekly).

■ You then look to where you can "piggyback" very similar products onto the fixed cycle for the green products. For example, the products may actually be identical, but differentiation between them occurs off the main production line, or perhaps the only difference is a change in pack print or label. These products can then be built into the fixed production cycle.

For the remaining products, there are a number of strategies that may be needed to fit them into the product cycle:

■ Applying focused Lean improvements such as setup time reduction to enable "yellow" products to be economically integrated into the product cycle.

---

* Glenday, I. 2006. *Breaking through to Flow: Banish Firefighting and Produce to Customer Demand.* Brookline, MA: Lean Enterprise Institute.

† Glenday, I. and Sather, R. 2013. *Lean RFS: Putting the Pieces Together.* New York: Productivity Press.

Table 6.2 Example of Product Mix Analysis

Cumulative % of Sales	Cumulative % of Product Range	Color Code
50	6	Green
95	50	Yellow
99	70	Blue
Last 1	30	Red

Source: Reprinted from Glenday, I., *Breaking through to Flow: Banish Firefighting and Produce to Customer Demand*, Lean Enterprise Institute, Brookline, MA, 2006.

■ Taking steps to reduce unnecessary complexity, such as harmonizing similar raw materials, packaging, parts, or subassemblies so that very similar products can be merged into a single product.

■ Phasing out very low-volume "red" and "blue" products where possible. A good tactic here can be giving a signal to customers, such as a higher price or longer lead time, to encourage them to purchase the "standard" product.

■ Finding alternative ways to produce low-volume products when they cannot be phased out. This might mean outsourcing these red or blue products or even creating a separate highly flexible production line for "make-to-order" low-volume products.

Once you have decided the products that you want to include in the cycle, then you can work out your product cycle. The steps to doing this are to

■ Decide the length of the cycle (ideally, one day or less and never more than one week).

■ Calculate the available production capacity over that period.

■ Develop the optimum cycle.

Creating the optimum cycle depends a lot on your process. However, by establishing a standard product cycle, you have the opportunity to run your production in the best sequence to optimize your production process. For example, in a beverage filling process, the most difficult and complex changeover might be a bottle size change, and the next most difficult a flavor change, followed by a label change and then a multipack carton change. Therefore, the sequence for the cycle might be

1. Run all the different carton variants for a given bottle size, label print, and flavor (e.g., 10 pack, 12 pack, 24 pack, etc.).
2. Run all the different label variants for a given bottle size and flavor (and for each label variant, run all the different multipack sizes).
3. Run all the different flavors for a given bottle size.
4. Change bottle size and start again.

This cycle enables the plant to cycle through its full product cycle while minimizing the most difficult changeovers.

In fact, in many factories there are multiple production lines. The opportunity then arises to build multiple production cycles by line. Therefore, to extend the beverage example, if our highest-volume size was 600 ml soda bottles, we might dedicate a production line to that product alone. We would then look to fill the next production line with our next highest-volume products, and finally might end up with a "short-run" production line where we run the remainder of our product range. Often, when I look at how factories are planned, scheduling is fairly random, with any product being potentially scheduled on any line. This clearly means that the opportunity to optimize a particular line for a particular product or range of products is lost. The use of product cycles to create "dedicated lines" overcomes this and can lead to large improvements in efficiency and throughput.

Running the Cycle

Ian Glenday calls his approach repetitive flexible supply (RFS) because he would argue that it offers both the benefits of routine and repetition, as well as flexibility to meet customer demand.

Once you have built the cycle, then the concept is to follow this cycle strictly. That means that every day or week (however long the cycle is), the *same quantity* of each product is manufactured in the *same sequence* every cycle. In doing this, you create "economics of repetition," where production teams gain efficiencies through following the same routine day after day and week after week. In the beverage filling example, I have mentioned that every morning might start with 500 ml bottles of lemonade and every evening finish with 600 ml bottles of cola. This kind of routine clearly makes a factory easier to run because not only do operators know exactly what they need to do every day, but the warehouse knows which materials to deliver and suppliers know what orders to expect. This predictability gives you a much greater chance of having the right materials in the right place when you need them.

Your regular schedule is going to produce the same products in the same quantities every cycle. You then use inventory as a buffer to allow for variations in actual customer demand, because customers don't buy the same products in the same quantities every cycle. You may need to use your sales and operations planning process (Chapter 5) to adjust the quantity of inventory or fine-tune the product cycle to allow for seasonal variation or promotions.

Leveling the Product Mix

I have talked quite a bit about changeover time as a driver of the need to run a regular product cycle. It is important to remember that running products in a regular cycle also has the effect of leveling your product mix. This minimizes fluctuations in output from running all the products with shorter cycle times followed by all the products with long cycle times. Ideally, you want to alternate the production of short and long cycle time products so that over the course of a production cycle, these variations in cycle time between products are leveled out.

Product Wheels

The RFS approach is a very specific approach to developing a regular product cycle. The key feature of RFS is that you produce the same products in the same sequence and the same quantities *every* cycle. The variation in demand is managed through having a finished goods inventory buffer. Ian Glenday is a good friend and a very effective evangelist for his RFS approach; however, in some cases it is very difficult to implement such a rigid product cycle. This is where the product range is large and changing. It can also happen in make-to-order production.

However, like RFS, there may be a natural cycle for the products where downtime can be reduced significantly by scheduling them in that cycle. In these situations, you can try a product wheel. Like RFS, you set a period for the production cycle, typically one day or one week, and a preferred sequence, but the quantity of product made in each cycle depends on the actual customer requirements.

To explain, I will use an example from an industry I worked in for many years. In plastics master batch extrusion,* there is a lot of benefit from scheduling products in a color sequence from light to dark. This is because the dark colors will generally cover over the lighter colors. As a result, making a color change from white to yellow is much easier than a change from black to white. However, most master batch plants manufacture thousands of different colors, each customized for a customer application. Creating a fixed product cycle using RFS principles is not really feasible for this type of product. In this case, you could create a product wheel, and this wheel would "rotate" daily, because master batch is a high service business. Figure 6.5 illustrates the likely production sequence in this type of product wheel.

In this example, the extruder output is 200 kg/h and the average order size is 200 kg. A simple changeover takes 20 minutes and a major clean (black to white) takes 1 hour. Therefore, in 24 hours you allow for one major clean, leaving 23 hours to run the product cycle and changeovers. An average batch takes 60 minutes to run and 20 minutes to changeover, and therefore you can run approximately 17 batches of average size per day. This equates to 3400 kg of output per day. Therefore, you can create the daily schedule. You accumulate orders in the sequence you receive them from the customer. Once 3400 kg worth of orders has been accumulated, you then arrange those orders into the ideal production cycle or "product wheel" in order of color. This then becomes the daily plan for the following day.

Using this product wheel approach provides a consistent output and lead time and minimizes changeovers. Compared with the RFS approach, it does not fully deliver the economics of repetition since the product cycle is different every day. However, it does provide some sense of routine and consistency, and therefore is a useful option, especially for make-to-order production, where it is not possible to hold an inventory buffer.

Summary

The question of what product to make next has been made incredibly complex due to the use of advanced software tools and supply chain theory. The

---

* Master batches are concentrated blends of plastic and pigments. Plastics molders will blend a small amount of master batch (usually less than 5%) with natural plastic beads in order to mold a colored product.

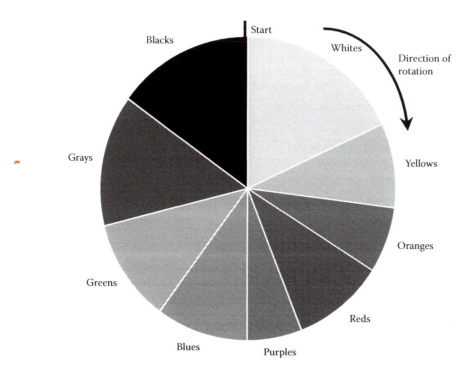

Figure 6.5   Example of a product wheel for plastics extrusion.

result is often confusion, poor on-time, in-full performance, and expediting to meet customer orders.

In a Lean production system, planning is very simple. Orders are released at one point in the process only, called the pacemaker process. Orders always flow downstream of the pacemaker in the sequence they are released, while production upstream is triggered by "pull" signals from the pacemaker.

We release work at the pacemaker at a regular interval called the pitch. This interval is a multiple of takt time and is often determined using a logical grouping of products, such as a pack or pallet of finished goods or a batch or customer order.

It is vital to *only* plan at the pacemaker. If you attempt to reschedule production at multiple points in the process, the result will be inconsistent lead times and, again, a collapse in your regular scheduling process.

For many processes, scheduling is as simple as following the sequence in which products are ordered. However, some degree of intervention in the sequence of production is often necessary to minimize long changeover times or to level out the product mix between products with different cycle times. To achieve this, we typically build a standard product sequence and arrange orders into this sequence for release at the pacemaker. Very simple tools such as RFS can be used to create this standard product sequence and ensure consistent delivery at minimum cost. Expediting can then be eliminated. The common thread of RFS and other scheduling tools is that the planning cycles need to be short (one week or less), and discipline needs to be applied to follow the sequence. Once the planning cycle gets longer, the pressure will always come to break out of the cycle, and this will lead you very quickly back to full-time expediting and firefighting.

Planning does not need to be complex to be successful. The many electronic scheduling tools available on the market look very impressive, but this does not mean that they work better or even as well as the simple Lean techniques described above. My experience, over my three decades in manufacturing, is that the Lean approach using simple tools such as the load leveling box in Figure 6.4 is the most effective approach to production scheduling. It is more likely to deliver to your customers the products they need on time and in full—and is much cheaper to implement than software!

Chapter 7

Managing Your Inbound Supply Chain

What You Will Learn in This Chapter

- *Why poor supplier performance is usually **not** the reason why you have shortages*
- *How to work out the right level of material inventory*
- *The key reasons why raw material shortages occur and how to take action to reduce your risk of shortages*
- *What just-in-time supply is and how it works*

This chapter focuses on sourcing materials for production. However, most distribution businesses purchase their goods from suppliers, and therefore the principles also apply to distributors.

If you have made it this far through this book, you should have the makings of an effective fulfillment system to meet your customer's needs on time, in full every time.

- From Chapter 2, you will have a good understanding of your supply chain and some ideas about how you might reduce your lead time by eliminating non-value-added time.
- From Chapter 3, you will have a high-level forecast, showing your overall demand trends without deceiving you into thinking that you can meet your day-to-day and week-to-week customer needs through complete reliance on a forecast.

- From Chapter 4, your sales and operations planning process will enable you to plan capacity to meet expected demand over the coming months, ensuring you have the people, productive capacity, and materials to meet the ups and downs of customer demand.
- From Chapter 5, you will have worked out your finished goods strategy and the level of finished goods inventory needed to ensure that you always have inventory available when your customers need it.
- Finally, Chapter 6 will have helped you established a simple and effective system for production scheduling based on releasing orders to a single pacemaker process.

It all sounds just about perfect. Nothing could go wrong. Then you run out of a key material* and will have to wait weeks to get more stock. All your careful plans now go out the window. You cannot complete production until the materials arrive, and as a result, the partly completed products get pulled off the production line and pushed aside to wait for the missing materials. Your sales team gets the unenviable task of calling the customer to explain why they will not get their products on time.

I have never done a survey of this, but anecdotally, I have seen enough businesses over the years to believe that material shortages are the number one cause of production schedule changes across almost every type of business, and therefore one of the largest causes of poor on-time, in-full delivery.

Unfortunately, material shortages often set off a "domino effect" of problems. The lack of a key material means that we cannot progress production on the first product on our schedule. Therefore, we have to interrupt production of this product or skip it all together and go to the next product. This will bring forward the production of this second product and, in doing, so bring forward the demand for materials required for that product. This may trigger another shortage if some of the materials for the second product have not yet been delivered. By the time the materials for the interrupted products finally arrive, they are probably already late for delivery and the customer will need urgent delivery. As a result, production will be interrupted again

---

* The term *raw material* is often used in continuous manufacturing such as food or chemicals. In discrete manufacturing, *parts* or *components* is often the term used to describe externally sourced materials. I have chosen to use the terms *materials* for consistency, but I am referring to all materials sourced from suppliers, whichever industry you are in and whatever you choose to call them. For distributors, the items they source will be finished goods; however, the principles behind reducing shortages are the same for distributors as well, although you will not have the benefit of being able to level your demand for materials.

(most likely disrupting the carefully designed product wheel you developed after Chapter 6) to reschedule and run the delayed products.

If you are a distribution business, I suspect that the examples above sound similar to the excuses you might hear from your suppliers when they do not deliver.

So Why Do Material Shortages Occur?

The obvious response might be that "suppliers let us down." The reality is that the solution is much more likely to arise in your own business than in your suppliers' business. In most basic terms, shortages occur because the quantity of materials used during the period from one delivery of materials to the next exceeds the quantity of materials held in inventory. This can occur for two reasons. Either the quantity of inventory is too low, or the usage is much greater than expected.

Two key factors determine the risk of a shortage. If the time between one delivery and the next (the replenishment interval) is long, then the risk of running out between deliveries increases. This is because the longer you have to wait for your next delivery, the greater the chance that you will experience unexpected demand and use up all your material inventory. The second factor is the lead time from when you place your order on your supplier to when you receive your goods. The longer the lead time, the earlier you will need to place the order to receive the goods in time. Given the limitations of forecasting discussed in Chapter 3, the further out you have to forecast your demand, the less accurate that forecast will be. Therefore, the longer the supplier lead time, the earlier you will need to order the materials you need and greater the chance that when they finally arrive, they will not be the right quantity. Pull systems also rely on the fact that material inventory you have just consumed is a good predictor of what you will use next. However, the longer the lead time, the less likely this will be the case, increasing the risk that the inventory that you have "pulled" is not what you will need when it finally arrives.

Based on this simple root cause analysis, the key to reducing shortages is therefore to shorten the supplier lead time, reduce the replenishment interval (order more frequently), and minimize the variability of demand and supply so that you can avoid shortages with minimum inventory.

In Chapter 5, we discussed finished goods inventory and learned that inventory exists to allow for the fact that customers do not always order the same amount every day and every week, and that supply is not always on time. The same applies at the other end of your supply chain with inventory of materials. Your inventory needs to allow for variation in usage of materials, as well as for variation in supply from your suppliers. The difference is that demand from your customer for finished goods is *independent* demand, which means that the demand for one product is generally not dependent on the demand for any other product. Demand for materials is instead *dependent* demand, in that the demand for materials depends on demand for the products that those materials are used in. For inventory of finished goods, the amount of variation in what you sell is largely in the hands of your customers. However, for supply of materials, you can influence the amount of variation in demand. By applying the techniques outlined in Chapter 5, you will use inventory or time buffers to reduce the impact of variable customer demand. Then scheduling a regular amount of production at a regular pitch interval and leveling product mix using "every part every interval" scheduling or "repetitive flexible supply" will make your demand for materials much more consistent and predictable. As a result, you can achieve a much lower level of material inventory than you need for finished goods.

Many businesses will aim to fix material shortages first before trying to implement level production. Unfortunately, this can prove an impossible challenge. Often, the instability of their production process is the major cause of their shortages. As a result, most Lean experts will suggest that you start at the customer and work backwards, stabilizing the supply of finished goods to the customer first, probably at the expense initially of some extra inventory. You then stabilize the production process and finally material supply. In practice, if the supply problem is bad, you may have to address all three areas at once in order to stabilize your supply chain.

Deciding the Right Level of Material Inventory

To work out the best way to manage materials, you can use a *plan for every part* (PFEP). This is described in detail in an excellent book, *Making Materials Flow*.* A PFEP is essentially a table (usually a spreadsheet) listing

---

* Harris, R., Harris, C. and Wilson, E. 2003. *Making Materials Flow: A Lean Material-Handling Guide for Operations, Production-Control, and Engineering Professionals*. Cambridge, MA: Lean Enterprise Institute.

each material and the key characteristics of that material. This includes physical characteristics, such as the type, size, and weight of products and packaging; supply chain characteristics, such as the minimum order quantity, supplier details, and lead time; and details about the usage of the part, including its average and maximum usage.

Calculating the correct level of raw material inventory is similar to the method used for finished goods.

$$Reorder\ point = Average\ usage + Safety\ stock$$

The safety stock allows for variation in demand and supply of the material. You can calculate this using the same formulas used to calculate the safety stock for finished goods in Chapter 5.

$$Safety\ stock = Z \times \sqrt{\left(\left(\frac{LT}{I} \times \sigma_D^2\right) + \left(\sigma_{LT} \times D_{AVG}\right)^2\right)}$$

In the case of materials,

- LT is the replenishment lead time from when you order the materials until they are in your location ready to use.
- I is the replenishment interval, in this case average frequency at which the material is ordered.
- σ_D is the standard deviation of your usage of the material.
- σ_{LT} is the standard deviation of your supplier's lead time.
- D_{AVG} is your average usage over the replenishment interval.

However, for materials demand is dependent on your consumption, and this can lead to quite "lumpy" demand for materials, especially low-usage materials that are only used in a few finished goods. For example, a particular material may have an annual usage of 4 units per month. You calculate your average usage of one unit per week (approximately) and your standard deviation is also one unit. If you target 98% availability and refer to Table 5.1, your Z score would be two standard deviations, which when added to your average usage gives you a target inventory of three units. However, this particular material is only used in one finished product, and each time you make that finished product, you use 10 units. If your target material inventory is only three units, you are going to have a shortage every time you make that product. In this case, you need to make sure that your inventory buffer considers the *maximum* likely usage of that raw material rather than simply using the *Z* score and standard deviation of usage. Therefore, for calculating inventory for materials, you often need to understand the consumption patterns in more detail, rather than simply calculating a standard deviation.

Why Do Shortages Occur?

So what are the key drivers of raw material shortages, and how do you address them? There are three key risk factors for raw material shortages:

1. Replenishment interval and quantity: Receiving smaller quantities more frequently will reduce risk of shortages.
2. Replenishment lead time.
3. Supply and demand variability.

If your goal is to reduce raw material shortages, then you should aim to reduce all three risk factors.

Reducing the Replenishment Interval

The first strategy to improve your raw material availability is to increase the frequency at which you order your materials and reduce the interval between orders, the replenishment interval. This means that instead of having to wait for a month between deliveries of a key material, you may receive orders every week or every few days. The effect of this is to reduce the risk of shortages, because the magnitude of usage variation will be less the shorter the replenishment interval. It will also reduce the consequences of a shortage, because the time from running out until receiving replacement stock is reduced. Reducing the replenishment interval means reducing quantities you are ordering. Therefore, you need to challenge why you are ordering these quantities. In many cases, the reasons for ordering large amounts can be quite trivial, such as

■ *"We have always ordered once a month."*
■ *"It saves work raising purchase orders."*

Often, suppliers apply minimum order quantities and charge more for small amounts; however, in many cases I find that companies just assume these supplier "rules" without ever testing them. In fact, when you place the order for an amount that is below the "minimum," the supplier will often happily continue to supply at the same price, no questions asked. If this does not occur, then you need to discuss with your supplier the reasons for applying a minimum quantity and see whether there are ways to preserve the suppliers' efficiency while reducing your order quantities. For example, many suppliers will be happy to hold some inventory of your parts and allow you to call off this inventory in small amounts, provided that you are committed to take this inventory within some agreed period. From the supplier's viewpoint, this inventory then gives them some freedom when they schedule production of your products, as they will be just replenishing inventory rather than having to meet an order deadline. It may be that the savings the supplier gets from running a product cycle (such as described in Chapter 6) outweighs the cost of holding inventory for you. Therefore, it is worth asking your supplier whether they would prefer to hold inventory for you.

Freight costs can also be a reason given for ordering large quantities, but in many cases, these assumptions can be flat wrong; that is, there are no extra freight costs for ordering a smaller amount. For example, there is rarely, if ever, freight savings in transporting more than one shipping container at once. However, I have known companies to place monthly or quarterly orders for up to 20 containers of materials at once. This represents a massive business risk should the shipment be delayed. Far better to order the containers once a week or even once a day to level out supply and ensure that the delay of any one shipment will have minimal impact.

In other cases, the additional freight costs are far outweighed by the savings in inventory holding costs that are achieved by ordering less. Freight costs can also be reduced by ordering "mixed loads." That is, rather than ordering a full pallet or a container load of a single item, consolidate all the different items you require into a single pallet or shipping container and order this. That way, you are paying the freight for a full load, but only ordering small quantities of each item.

Moving to a *fixed-interval, variable-quantity* delivery model can help address freight costs. This means that instead of ordering each product individually as a requirement is triggered, you place an order with each key supplier at a regular interval for *all* the items that might need replenishment at that point in time.

Using the reorder point replenishment model described above can also lead to excessively high inventory, when the replenishment lead time is long. As discussed in Chapter 5, for a reorder point model of replenishment to work, the reorder quantity must always be greater than the reorder point. Therefore, for items where the reorder quantity is high, it makes sense to go to a Kanban system, where multiple replenishment orders can be in process at any one time. This is described in more detail in Chapter 5. For replenishment of materials, sending physical Kanban cards to your suppliers may not be feasible; therefore, you can maintain a "virtual" Kanban system on a spreadsheet or track the status of Kanban orders on a Kanban control board such as Figure 7.1. In this example, the hooks where Kanban cards are hung represent the products that are currently on order, while the empty hooks are items where there is currently sufficient stock. The big advantage of using Kanban over a simple reorder point system is that you now have multiple replenishment orders in process leading, to more frequent orders of smaller quantities, and therefore reducing your replenishment interval and risk of shortage.

Using some of the strategies outlined above, you should reduce the order quantities and the replenishment interval for many of your materials to the smallest amount that is economically and practically achievable. You will find that the more frequently you order your materials, the lower your risk of shortages.

Figure 7.1 Example of a Kanban control board. As materials are consumed, Kanban cards are returned to purchasing, triggering ordering. The cards then stay on this board until the materials are delivered, and then the card is removed and attached to the new material containers.

Reducing Supplier Lead Time

The second big lever on reducing supply chain risk is reducing supplier lead time. That is the time from when you place an order until you receive your goods. This is independent of the replenishment interval. To reduce supplier lead time, you need to understand what makes up the lead time. The most effective way to do this is with a value stream map. In this value stream map, your business is the customer and you work your way back from there. The information flow starts with your process for internally triggering replenishment, and you need to consider your own internal processes for converting this into demand on the supplier in the form of a purchase order or Kanban signal. This is important, as I have identified delays in some businesses of several days from when replenishment is triggered in the plant until the supplier actually gets the order to supply that stock.

The level of detail that you can build into your supplier value stream map will depend on the level of access and cooperation that your supplier will provide you. Ideally, you would have supplier representatives involved in the value stream mapping workshops and the mapping would include the supplier's internal processes. If this is not possible, you may find that the supplier is simply a "process box" on your value stream. Nevertheless, it is worth mapping this simple value stream, as it will show the information flows between your business and the supplier. It will show the inputs to your supplier and how they influence your supplier's process. It will also show the freight and logistics connections between the supplier and your business, and it should show the deployment of inventory between your supplier and your business.

Several years ago, I mapped the material ordering process for a major high-technology manufacturer. This manufacturer was ordering thousands of different materials, and was suffering more than 100 shortages per day. When we mapped the supply value stream (Figure 7.2), we discovered one of the key root causes of the problem. Suppliers were allowed an eight-day lead time to supply, but two to three days of this was consumed internally with order processing and receiving at the manufacturer. From when a requirement for a material was triggered, it took 24–36 hours before the supplier actually received the order due to delays in manually approving and faxing the order. Then once the goods arrived on site, they might wait a further 24–36 hours before being received into inventory and delivered to location. In our future state shown in Figure 7.3, we automated the process of sending orders so they were sent to the supplier as soon as the requirement was

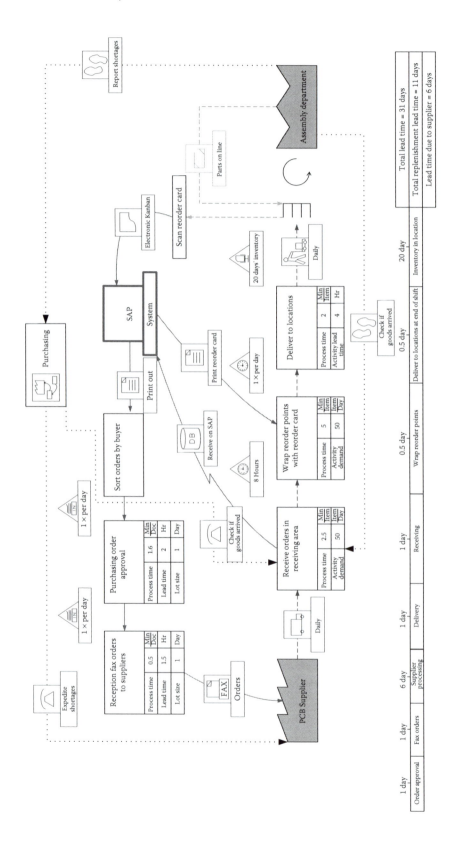

Figure 7.2 This current state value stream map of supply of printed circuit boards (PCBs) identified that almost half of the supply lead time was due to delays in the order processing and receiving processes.

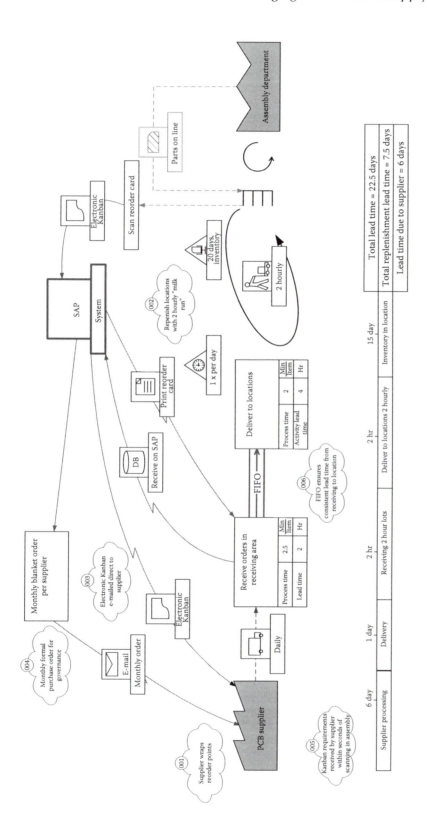

Figure 7.3   By sending electronic Kanban signals directly to the supplier and simplifying the receiving process, both lead time and inventory were significantly reduced in the future state. PCB, printed circuit board.

triggered in assembly. We also streamlined the receiving process by setting
lead time targets, having suppliers pack reorder points, and replenishing
locations through the day rather than at the end of the shift. This reduced the
internal lead times from 48–72 hours down to around 4 hours, significantly
reducing the risk of shortages.

As this example shows, delays you create yourself in your order handling
process are often the easiest to eliminate.

Once you have reduced your order processing lead time, you can then
look at ways to reduce your supplier's lead time. Your ability to do this will
depend on the depth into which you are able to work with your supplier to
understand and improve their process. Some of the tactics that you and your
supplier may apply to reduce lead time may include

- Establishing Lean processes, including a dedicated production cell in
  your supplier's factory to reduce their internal lead time.
- Putting in place a pull system (Kanban system) to trigger the supply of
  inventory to your plant.
- Removal of links in the transport supply chain, for example, eliminating
  intermediate warehousing, eliminating cross-docking steps, having the
  supplier deliver direct to your production line, or even having the supplier replenish the storage location on your line (this is quite common
  with suppliers of consumable items or fasteners).
- Becoming more predictable in your ordering by establishing a routine
  ordering pattern and leveling your demand. Once the supplier understands your regular demand pattern, it becomes easier for them to align
  their production scheduling and material ordering to meet your demand.

Reducing Demand and Supply Variability

The third factor that will impact whether you run out of materials is the
amount of variability in demand and supply. On the demand side, the way
that your business ensures stable demand for materials is by having a stable
production schedule. The system we outlined in Chapter 6 will ensure that
you produce at a constant rate and follow a regular production cycle. This
will then mean that you consume materials in a very predictable and consistent way. This is a huge benefit to your suppliers and will enable you
to reduce material inventory over time. This is because the regular cycle

enables you to accurately predict what you will need each day or week. You are also likely to reduce the risk of shortages since suppliers will be able to plan with confidence to supply you the materials you need for each production cycle, knowing it will be the same as the last production cycle.

Once you have mapped and understood your supply chain and know you have a stable consumption pattern delivering stable, consistent demand on suppliers, the remaining variability in supply can be isolated to your supplier's performance. We will discuss the ways to effectively manage your supplier relationship and supplier performance in Chapter 9; however, it is important to realize that the start point is to have a discussion with your supplier to understand the potential reasons for their unreliability. In the meantime, it is advisable to increase your inventory of the problem supplier's materials or ask them to increase the inventory they hold on your behalf. This inventory buffer will act as a "firewall" between your process, your customers, and your supplier's problems.

In Chapter 8, we will look at a particular category of materials that feature in almost every business's supply chain and which present a particular set of challenges—materials that are sourced from overseas.

Summary

Material shortages are typically the largest single cause of on-time, in-full delivery failures. Unfortunately, many companies simply blame their suppliers for this, when it is often failings in their own processes that provide the root causes for many of these shortages. To reduce material shortages, there are a number of key steps:

1. Ensure you have the right amount of material inventory. The stock calculation formulas in Chapter 5 can also be used for calculating material inventory. However, you have to also remember that material demand depends on your usage of those materials, so you need to factor in the known characteristics of that usage rather than simply apply the formula.
2. Reduce the replenishment interval: Purchasing materials in smaller quantities more often will reduce your inventory and reduce your risk of shortage.
3. Reduce the replenishment lead time: Use a value stream map and work with your suppliers to understand the key drivers of lead time. Often, they are factors within your business's control.

4. Reduce demand and supply variability. By ordering a regular amount in a regular pattern, you will make it easier for your supplier to meet your demand reliably. Leveling and stabilizing your production rate and product mix using the techniques outlined in Chapter 6 will result in more consistent demand for materials, making it easier for your suppliers to meet your demand on time and in full every time.

Chapter 8

Making Your International Supply Chain Work

What You Will Learn in This Chapter

International suppliers are part of almost every manufacturing or distribution supply chain today. Unfortunately, many companies face high costs and high inventory and still achieve poor on-time, in-full delivery from their international suppliers. This chapter unravels why and provides some practical ideas to improve the operation of your international supply chain, including

- *How to reduce the lead time in your international supply chain*
- *Reducing inventory and risk in your international supply chain by increasing shipping frequency*
- *How to use repetitive flexible replenishment to simplify and streamline your international supply chain*
- *How to manage low-volume items from international suppliers*
- *How to assess the total costs for your overseas sourced materials and products and compare them with those of locally sourced alternatives*

Over the past 20 years, almost every manufacturing and distribution business has been connected to the global supply chain. Most businesses now source a significant proportion of their materials from other parts of the world. This has provided a huge challenge for companies attempting to deliver on time, in full to their customers.

As a general rule, the farther away you source a material from, the longer it will take you to get that product. This is pretty obvious. It should take much longer to get a key material from China or India than it does from the factory next door. I say "should" because I am constantly frustrated by suppliers who offer their customers excessively long lead times and eliminate any competitive advantage from being "local." As explained above, if the lead time to obtain the material is much longer because it is coming from the other side of the world, then you will need to order it much earlier in order to have the material on time for you to meet your customer's delivery deadline. In fact, in most cases you are going to have to order your materials from your overseas suppliers well before your customer has even ordered their products from you. Therefore, you are going to need to rely on a forecast of the expected demand from the customer. We discussed in Chapter 3 that the longer your forecast horizon, the less accurate your forecast will be. As a result, you will need to carry inventory of the imported material, and the longer the lead time from overseas, the more inventory you will need to carry. As well, the further out you have the forecast, the greater the likely magnitude of any errors in that forecast and the greater the chance that the forecast will underestimate demand and you will run out of materials. Therefore, in summary, the longer the lead time from your overseas supplier, the more inventory you need to carry and the greater the chance that even this higher level of inventory will not be enough and you will run out and fail to deliver on time, in full.

In addition, goods get shipped around the world in bulk. There are usually large freight cost savings to be made by buying whole shipping containers full of product rather than purchasing in smaller quantities. This tends to lead to infrequent deliveries of large amounts of product.

Finally, the vagaries of international trade can mean that port delays, customs clearances, quarantine issues, ships' captains who decide to arbitrarily offload your cargo, and any number of other events can impact your shipment.

The three big drivers of shortages—long lead times, infrequent deliveries, and supply variability—are writ large in international trade.

So how do you effectively manage an import supply chain in order to minimize shortages while minimizing inventory? Over the years, I have assisted several companies with this challenge and have come up with a simple, step-by-step process to improve the operation of the international supply chain. This focuses on the three main levers for reducing shortages—reducing the lead time, increasing the replenishment frequency, and reducing variability.

Table 8.1   Shipping Lead Times between Major International Ports[a]

Departure Port	Arrival Port	Loading Time	Shipping Time	Unloading and Clearance Time	Total Lead Time
Shanghai	Melbourne	2 days	13 days	3 days	18 days
Shanghai	Hamburg	2 days	25 days	3 days	30 days
Shanghai	Los Angeles	2 days	13 days	3 days	18 days
Rotterdam	Melbourne	2 days	37 days	3 days	42 days
Felixstowe	Singapore	2 days	21 days	3 days	26 days

[a] You can obtain shipping schedules between any two ports in the world using websites such as www.linescape.com.

Reducing the Lead Time in an International Supply Chain

I live in Australia, and it is not unusual for companies sourcing raw materials from Asia to accept lead times of 12–20 weeks from order to delivery, and even longer lead times are common when sourcing from the United States or Europe. However, what should the lead time be? As I discuss in Chapter 7, the start point to reducing supply lead time is to map the supply chain using a value stream map. In the case of an international supply chain, this becomes even more important, because the lead time is longer and there are usually many more links in the supply chain. One surprising fact you will find, however, is that the amount of time your products spend actually traveling around the world on board a ship or transiting ports is usually only a small proportion of the total lead time you experience when ordering goods from overseas. Modern container ships are fast, and ports are increasingly efficient. Key shipping lines often run several services a week between key ports, a bit like train schedules.

As you can see from Table 8.1, the actual lead time from port to port for most international shipping routes is less than four weeks. So why are lead times for imported goods so long? There are many reasons for this, but some of the more common ones are shown in Table 8.2.

Increasing Shipment Frequency and Reducing Variability

For international supply chains, you want to ship products as frequently as possible and level the demand on your suppliers. Unfortunately, the fact that goods are typically shipped internationally in large containers mean that many companies will accumulate their demand until they require a full container

Table 8.2 Common Causes of Excessive Order Delays and Countermeasures to Address Them

Delay	Countermeasure
Goods waiting at the port for the ship	Develop a regular ordering schedule around a regular shipping schedule (perhaps with the same shipper). Orders should be placed, processed, and delivered to port to be just-in-time to meet the ship.
Suppliers waiting for your order until they order raw materials	Provide suppliers some certainty in the form of a rolling monthly forecast (making sure that they cannot make the whole year's forecast at once).
Suppliers consolidate your orders to run big batches	Ensure your service level agreement prohibits suppliers from delaying orders to consolidate with later orders.
Long clearance delays	Get your freight forwarder to use preclearance procedures if necessary. Ensure that manifests are accurate and all clearance and quarantine procedures are complied with.
Cross-docking delays	Simplify the supply chain by opting for direct freight routes where possible. Reduce the number of supply chain players by considering a single logistics provider to handle the end-to-end freight and logistics from your supplier's door to yours.
Order processing delays	Standardize ordering procedures where possible to streamline approvals and prepayment processes.

load (FCL) of a particular material before they order. This can mean that suppliers see no demand for weeks or even months and then are suddenly hit with a very large order. Obviously, when this occurs it is unlikely that suppliers will have materials ready or be able to easily schedule in production, adding to delays. On the other hand, ordering small quantities in part containers will most likely add significantly to freight costs and add to lead times, as goods will need to go to a cross-dock facility to be consolidated into containers with other people's goods and then on arrival will have to be cross-docked again to separate your goods out of the container for delivery.

To overcome this problem, I have used a version of the repetitive flexible supply scheduling method described in Chapter 6. I call it "repetitive flexible replenishment."

In Chapter 7, we discussed developing a plan for every part (PFEP). This is a spreadsheet with one line for every material that you purchase.

It records data such as usage, packaging type, supplier name, order quantity, and inventory levels. For international supply chains, you need to add additional columns to your PFEP for the city where your supplier is located, the most convenient shipping port for that supplier to ship your materials through, and your average usage in number of pallets. Start with one key supplier. Rank the materials you source from them according to the total number of pallets required over a year (or a season in the case of a seasonal product). Divide this by the number of months and weeks to get a number of pallets per month, week, or day in the case of really high-volume products. You will also need to know the number of pallets that can fit in a shipping container. Typically, 20–40 pallets fit in a 40-foot shipping container, depending on the pallet height and whether the pallets can be double stacked, but if your pallets are irregularly sized, this may differ. If you divide the number of pallets per container by the average total material usage in pallets per day, you can calculate the number of days per shipping container. This should be a combined total of *all* the materials purchased from that supplier. This is your replenishment interval for that product. Typically, we will round this to the nearest whole number of days or weeks. Try to avoid replenishment intervals of more than one month—I will describe how to do that later in this section.

Now look at your materials and apply the Glenday sieve as described in Chapter 6. How many pallets are required for each material in each interval? You will find that a few material numbers will represent the majority of pallets that you send each replenishment interval ("green" materials). Once you have calculated the quantity of pallets for these high-usage items, you need to set a fixed-order quantity where you order the same number of pallets of these key items *every* order interval. Changes to the quantity and frequency of ordering these high-volume materials should only occur in response to major changes in demand highlighted in your sales and operations planning process. Otherwise, week-to-week and day-to-day demand fluctuations for these materials should be buffered by having an appropriately sized inventory buffer of these materials. Fortunately, because you will have established a stable production process that operates at a regular pitch interval and has a regular product mix, demand for these materials will be very stable. Table 8.3 shows the Glenday sieve analysis for sheet metal parts for an Australian high-technology manufacturer we worked with. As you can see, 3 parts out of the 36 shown represent 50% of the total shipping volume. These parts represented 1366 pallets per year, or an average of 26 pallets per week. This represents more than half the capacity of a shipping container,

Table 8.3 Glenday Sieve Analysis of Sheet Metal Parts

Description	Forecast Annual Usage	Proposed Pack Quantity	Cartons per Pallet	Pallet Quantity	Pallets per Year	% of Total	Cumulative %
Assy frame welded large	704	1	1	1	704.0	33	33
Kit paint cover	1030	2	1	2	515.0	24	58
Assy cabinet ba	440	3	1	3	146.7	7	64
Assy base spect	1129	8	1	8	141.1	7	71
Assy optics sup	1367	12	1	12	113.9	5	76
Shield burner C	841	6	2	12	70.1	3	80
Panel lamp 4 WA	1030	15	1	15	68.7	3	83
Assy rf box wel	165	3	1	3	55.0	3	86
Shield burner C	238	10	1	10	23.8	1	87
Assy base ABC12	454	20	1	20	22.7	1	88
Assy cabinet TE	235	12	1	12	19.6	1	89
Cover RFbox com	703	36	1	36	19.5	1	90
Holder	457	24	1	24	19.0	1	91
Assy base trim	454	12	2	24	18.9	1	91
Bracket door st	1030	28	2	56	18.4	1	92
Assy cover switch	1129	32	2	64	17.6	1	93
Chassis cabinet	400	24	1	24	16.7	1	94

Assy fan baffle	1027	63	1	63	16.3	1	95
Bracket power s	1037	36	2	72	14.4	1	95
Assy baffle opt	1377	24	4	96	14.3	1	96
Panel divider G	1116	45	2	90	12.4	1	97
Bracket cover M	1259	27	4	108	11.7	1	97
Assy cover small	129	8	2	16	8.1	0	98
Assy housing PU	248	8	4	32	7.8	0	98
Tray sample	480	16	4	64	7.5	0	98
Assy cover B	129	10	2	20	6.5	0	99
Assy source MIR	1024	40	4	160	6.4	0	99
Assy ext sample	281	12	4	48	5.9	0	99
Assy D2 bracket	1014	48	4	192	5.3	0	99
Assy chassis EL	105	5	4	20	5.3	0	100
Assy cover lever	454	24	4	96	4.7	0	100
Plate M/switch	4798	102	75	7650	0.6	0	100
Mount mirror	4366	93	75	6975	0.6	0	100
Assy infill lh	841	18	75	1350	0.6	0	100
Tray drip	458	48	18	864	0.5	0	100
Assy panel door	1033	29	75	2175	0.5	0	100

so in this case, every weekly shipment contained the weekly quantity of these parts.

We recommend you set a target stock for these items that includes the total stock in the pipeline—stock on order, stock in transit, and stock in your warehouse. This can be controlled by a simple spreadsheet such as the one in Table 8.4. In this case, the replenishment lead time is seven weeks. This is made up of the current week's orders, three weeks of orders in production at the supplier, and three weeks on the water. The spreadsheet then predicts the stock level that will be in place each week for the seven-week cycle. Each week, the buyer completes the "new order on supplier" column and adjusts the quantity to keep the predicted inventory between the minimum and maximum levels. For many items, especially the high-volume items (the "greens" in Table 8.3), you can see that the order is fairly constant each week. However, for lower-volume parts, demand can vary and they may only be ordered every second week. When the total stock in the supply chain is predicted to fall below the minimum level, an additional order will be triggered, or when it is predicted to exceed the maximum, a weekly order may be skipped. This can also occur for materials where the standard carton quantity is not an exact match for the usage over the replenishment interval. Overall, the weekly ordering matches the weekly usage and provides very stable and predictable demand for suppliers. In our experience, suppliers then tend to organize themselves around this demand, meaning they are better prepared to respond to your orders. As a result, lead times tend to be shorter and unexpected delays fewer.

When your high-level forecast indicates a likely increase or decrease in demand, you can adjust for this simply by adjusting the minimum and maximum stock upward. This will give you a larger buffer for demand variation and pull in additional stock. If the increased demand is sustained initially, the system will trigger you to pull more product. You may want to also adjust your weekly order quantities; however, these are often related to standard carton and pallet quantities, and so often it may mean that you are going to occasionally pull twice in an order interval or skip a cycle, depending on whether the demand shift is up or down.

For lower-volume items, you will eventually get to a point where demand for a particular material over the replenishment interval is less than a carton. In this case, depending on the nature of the materials, you may choose to have a regular cycle for that material that is fortnightly or monthly.

In this regular replenishment cycle, the frequency of replenishment is much less than the lead time to replenishment. That is, the lead time from

Table 8.4 Example of a Simple Replenishment Tool for Imported Materials

Description	Weekly Usage	Proposed Pack Quantity	Minimum Stock	Maximum Stock	Stock on Hand	Shipments in Transit ETA 8/5/16	ETA 8/12/16	ETA 8/19/16	Future Seafreight Shipments ETD 8/3/16	ETD 8/10/16	ETD 8/17/16	New Order for Supplier ETD 8/24/16	Predicted Stock Levels 8-6-16	8-13-16	8-20-16	8-27-16	9-3-16	9-10-16	9-17-16
Assy frame welded large	13.5	1	42	95	28	14	14	28	14	14	14	14	28	29	43	44	44	43	43
Kit paint cover	19.8	2	60	140	78	20	20	20	20	20	20	20	78	78	79	79	79	79	79
Assy cabinet ba	8.5	3	27	60	22	9	9	15	9	9	9	9	23	23	30	30	31	31	32
Assy base spect	21.7	8	72	152	73	24	24	24	24	24	24	24	75	78	80	82	84	87	89
Assy optics sup	26.3	12	84	192	200	36	12	24	24	24	24	24	210	195	193	191	189	186	184
Shield burner C	16.2	6	54	114	48	18	18	18	18	18	18	18	50	52	53	55	57	59	61
Panel lamp 4 WA	19.8	15	60	150	44	30	30	30	30	30	30	30	54	64	75	85	95	105	115
Assy rf box wel	3.2	3	12	24	8	6	6	6	6	6	6		11	14	16	19	22	25	22
Shield burner C	4.6	10	20	40	35	10	12	10	10	10	6		40	36	41	37	42	38	33
Assy cabinet TE	4.5	6	24	36	5	12	12	12	6	6	6	6	12	20	27	29	30	32	33
Cover RFbox com	13.5	15	72	108	45	15	30	15	30	15	15	15	46	63	64	81	82	84	85
Holder	8.8	12	48	72	40	12	12	12	12	12	12	12	43	46	50	53	56	59	62
Assy base trim	8.7	12	36	72	46	12	12	12	12	12	12	12	49	53	56	59	62	66	69
Bracket door st	19.8	28	84	140	66	28	28	28	28	28	28	28	74	82	91	99	107	115	123
Chassis cabinet	7.7	12	24	72	77		12		12		12	28	69	74	66	70	63	67	59
Assy fan baffle	19.8	24	63	189	154	24	24	24	24	24	24	24	158	163	167	171	175	180	184
Bracket power s	19.9	24	72	144	154	24	24	24		24	24	24	158	138	142	122	126	106	110
Assy baffle opt	26.5	24	96	192	168	24	24	24	24	24	24	24	166	163	161	158	156	153	151
Panel divider G	21.5	24	90	180	96	24	24	24	24	24	24	24	99	101	104	106	109	111	114
Bracket cover M	24.2	27	81	189	135	27	27	27	27	27	27	27	138	141	143	146	149	152	155
Assy housing PU	4.8	6	16	40	25	6	6	6	6	6	6	6	26	27	29	30	31	32	34
Assy source MIR	19.7	24	80	160	66	24	24	24	24	24	24	24	70	75	79	83	88	92	96
Assy ext sample	5.4	6	24	48	36	6	6	6	6	6	6	6	37	37	38	38	39	40	40
Assy D2 bracket	19.5	24	96	144	88	24	24	24	24	24	24	24	93	97	102	106	111	115	120
Assy chassis EL	2.0	3	10	15	16	3	3	3		3		3	17	15	16	14	15	13	14
Plate M/switch	92.3	102	306	714	102	102	204	102	204	102	102	102	112	223	233	345	355	364	374
Mount mirror	84.0	93	279	651	186	93	93	93	93	186	93	93	195	204	213	222	324	333	342
Assy infill lh	16.2	18	54	126	72	18	18	18	18	18	18	18	74	76	77	79	81	83	85
Tray drip	8.8	16	48	96	50	16	16	16	16	16	16		57	64	72	79	86	93	84
Assy panel door	19.9	24	87	145	132	24	24	24	24	24	24	18	136	140	144	149	153	157	137

placing a particular order until receiving the materials might be 6–12 weeks; however, the time from receiving one delivery of the materials to the next will only be the replenishment interval. It is also likely with a long supply chain that you will have variable demand and supply. In the example in Table 8.4, we used the formula in Chapter 5 to calculate safety stock.

$$\text{Safety stock} = Z \times \sqrt{\left(\left(\frac{LT}{I} \times \sigma_D^2 \right) + \left(\sigma_{LT} \times D_{\text{AVG}} \right)^2 \right)}$$

If we choose the first product, "Assy frame welded large,"

Standard score = Z = 2.05 (we want to achieve 98% stock availability)
Replenishment lead time = LT = 7 weeks
Replenishment interval = I = 1 week
Average usage = D_{AVG} = 13.5
Standard deviation of demand = σ_D = 5 units
Standard deviation of lead time = σ_{LT} = 0.3 days

Therefore, safety stock is

$$\text{Safety stock} = 2.05 \times \sqrt{\left(\left(\frac{7}{1} \times 5^2 \right) + \left(0.3 \times 13.5 \right)^2 \right)}$$
$$= 28.4 \text{ units}$$

To calculate the minimum stock, we use

$$\text{Minimum stock} = \text{Average weekly usage} + \text{Safety stock}$$
$$= 13.5 + 28.4 = 41.9$$

In this case, the maximum stock was set at the replenishment lead time, or seven weeks, on the basis that there was never any point holding more than seven week's stock, as new stock could always be obtained within that lead time. Therefore, maximum stock was

$$\text{Maximum stock} = \text{Average weekly usage} \times \text{Replenishment lead time}$$
$$= 13.5 \times 7 = 94.5$$

A more scientific method could be used to calculate maximum stock; however, the main purpose of the replenishment spreadsheet shown in Table 8.4 was to avoid falling below the minimum stock, and so the maximum stock was set to simply prevent overstocking.

Consistent with Ian Glenday's repetitive flexible supply described in Chapter 6, this system assumes a constant rate of supply, with the inventory buffer allowing for variation in supply and demand. Larger demand swings (such as seasonality) that may occur over the lead time can greatly increase the demand variability, and therefore lead to the system calculating high levels of safety stock. The lower you can reduce the replenishment lead time, the less significant these demand swings will be and the less inventory you need to hold. If you cannot reduce the lead time, then you may need to allow for this longer-run demand variability by adjusting the minimum stock based on high and low season demand.

Options When Your Monthly Demand Does Not Fill a Container

Often, you will find that your usage of materials from a single overseas supplier is much less than a full shipping container per month. The first option is to consider ordering 20-foot containers rather than 40-foot containers. This immediately halves your order size, and while freight costs may increase slightly, it is still much cheaper and quicker than shipping individual pallets.

Another option is to look at your PFEP and group the materials by location. You may find that you have several suppliers located close to one another. In this case, you may consider talking to your freight forwarder and setting up a consolidation center at a port that is near to these suppliers. Each supplier would then ship their materials at regular intervals to the consolidation center. The materials from the different suppliers would then be consolidated into a single shipping container at the consolidation center for shipping direct to your site. This does add a consolidation step and some cost, but is generally cheaper and quicker than sending your freight in individual pallets as less than a container load (LCL) freight where it has to be cross-docked at each end of the supply chain.

A similar approach to having a consolidation center is to appoint one supplier as your "Tier 1" supplier responsible for consolidating and even sourcing the other materials from related nearby suppliers. This can be particularly effective if materials need to be kitted or assembled for use. By getting your supplier to perform this kitting or assembly, you not only simplify your supply chain, but also save time at your end.

Another problem you will face is that your order requirements for your weekly cycle may not exactly equal a whole number of containers. That is, what happens if your order equals 1.4 containers or 0.7 container? I have overcome this in a three ways. First, as recommended above, you should always try to level the quantity you order each cycle and use inventory at your end to buffer variations in your demand for the materials. Second, you can have business rules that allow for part container quantities to be rolled over to the next regular order cycle. This is quite complex in practice, as you need to decide which goods get left behind each time this happens, and you will also need to allow additional inventory for the risk that a shipment of a particular material will be delayed in this way. Third, you may choose to ship a partly filled container. As long as the goods are securely packed within the container (to prevent movement and damage), there is no reason why you have to fill every container to the maximum amount. Shipping a 70% filled container as a FCL is generally much cheaper than shipping the individual pallets as LCL. In fact, I typically would use all three strategies and have clear business rules that would determine whether a part container would be shipped or whether goods would be held over for the next shipment.

Managing Very Low-Volume Materials

Finally, you will get to very low-volume materials, where even a single carton may be months of stock. In this case, you would not schedule regular replenishment, but instead hold enough stock in your warehouse to cover the full replenishment lead time for that material from the supplier. When replenishment of that material is triggered, then there should be enough stock to cover the time to order it, source it, and have it delivered. This might be months of stock, but because the materials are very low volume, the inventory quantity involved is quite small. It can also pay to source these materials locally rather than internationally, as the inventory holding cost associated with sourcing them offshore may exceed the savings in unit costs. If the value of these low-volume items is quite high relative to their size and weight (e.g., pharmaceuticals or electronics), then it may be cheaper to hold a lower level of inventory and replenish them using airfreight.

Over the years, my colleagues at TXM and I have applied the repetitive flexible replenishment approach to a wide range of international supply chains. The result has always been the same: lower inventory, fewer shortages, and lower costs. However, as costs rise in the major Asian manufacturing hubs, especially China, it is perhaps time to reassess the sense of importing your materials.

Does Importing Still Make Sense? Assessing the Total Cost

This chapter has been mainly dedicated to helping you streamline and simplify your international supply chain to provide you with a more stable supply of your imported materials and reduce the risk of shortages. However, it may also be worthwhile to assess whether importing materials makes economic sense for your business at all.

Often, when decisions are made to source materials, the focus is on the unit cost of the goods. However, there are many other costs associated with importing goods compared with local supply (if you have a good local supplier). Obviously, goods sourced offshore need to be transported to their destination, so freight is a component that needs to be considered (and usually is). Beyond freight, a number of costs need to be factored in to make a true comparison of your imported alternative. These include

- Inventory holding costs: Inventory increases in proportion to lead time and replenishment interval. Therefore, the longer the supply chain, the more inventory that is required. You should calculate the inventory holding cost as the "interest" on the cash tied up in the additional inventory required to support your import supply chain (over and above what you would need to support local supply). This is usually higher than bank interest, as businesses fund their capital through a mix of bank debt and shareholders' equity and shareholders expect a much higher return than bank interest. For most businesses, this target return, known as the "weighted average cost of capital," is between 10% and 15%.
- Warehousing costs: These can be readily calculated for the additional inventory and may include additional handling costs if the additional inventory needs to be held in a separate warehouse.
- Cost of poor quality: Even if the quality you receive from your overseas supplier is equal to the local alternative, the costs of a quality problem will be much greater for imports. This is because quality problems are likely to be found at the end of the supply chain, when you or your customer first inspect or use the goods. By then, the whole supply chain, including inventory in the warehouse and goods in transit, is likely to be affected. At best, this inventory will need to be laboriously inspected; at worst, it will need to be scrapped and replacement inventory expedited at high cost from your supplier.
- Costs of supporting overseas suppliers: Think of the last time you took a whole week of your time to visit a supplier located around the corner

from your business. Of course, it is never necessary. However, establishing relationships with overseas suppliers and a properly functioning supply chain will require visits to the supplier's site, as well as ongoing monitoring. Even if you plan to outsource this to a consultant or agent, the ongoing costs can be considerable and are rarely counted into the cost of the goods.

■ Management of obsolescence: Product life cycles continue to get shorter. Over the past 30 years, the product life cycle for a television from product launch to discounting has reduced from three years to just three months. While consumer electronics and fashion are the best examples, many other industries have seen their product life cycles shrink. Managing the change from an old product to the new one becomes more and more difficult and costly the longer the supply chain. As well, the risk that the process won't happen smoothly and you will be left with obsolete stock after launch or (worse) a gap in supply is increased considerably the farther away your suppliers are.

■ Currency volatility and relative inflation: In recent years, this has been the largest factor impacting the costs of sourcing offshore. When companies make major business decisions, they often make these decisions in "today's dollars." In other words, exchange rate movements and inflation are not factored into the calculations, as they are seen as too difficult to predict. However, the fact that wages and the currency in China were going to rise in the last decade was highly predictable and was predicted by most economists. Unfortunately, many companies failed to factor this change into their outsourcing calculations, and I suspect that many now face costs that are actually higher than they started with before outsourcing (particularly when all the hidden costs listed above are taken into account).

These costs, when added up, can be considerable. In 2010, I modeled the total cost of sourcing custom sheet metal components from China. I found that even when the unit cost of a material sourced from China was 40% less than the unit cost of the same material sourced in Australia, the total cost of sourcing that material over five years was cheaper in Australia. I recently reviewed that analysis, given that we now know how exchange rates and inflation have changed over the past six years, and found that my 2010 prediction was almost exactly correct. Total cost for those materials sourced in China was significantly higher over five years than if they had been sourced locally. I also note that the client for whom I did that analysis (who chose to ignore this advice and outsourced their supply and production anyway) has recently started reshoring part of their production back to Australia.

Finally, in considering the merits of outsourcing, you need to return to the theme of the book. If you increase the lead time, reduce the frequency of replenishment, and increase the variability in the supply chain by sourcing from overseas, then you increase the risk of running out of key materials all together. When this happens, you will not be able to supply your customers what they want on time and in full. You will lose that sale, you may damage your customer's business, and ultimately, you risk destroying your relationship with your customer and permanently damaging your future business. Sourcing globally is now a part of almost every supply chain; however, it is timely to review your sourcing decisions and be completely sure that your low-cost foreign supplier is really the best option for your business and your customers.

Summary

After 20 years of globalization, international supply chains form part of almost every manufacturing or distribution company in the world. Sourcing key materials and products from around the world makes the goal of delivering what your customers need on time and in full significantly more challenging. It is always better and, in many cases, when total costs are considered, cheaper to source products and materials as close as possible to your market. However, when this is not possible and you need to source from far away, you can significantly improve delivery, while reducing inventory, by applying a few fairly straightforward techniques:

- Analyze your end-to-end supply chain using a value stream map for each key supply route or product family to see the drivers of lead time.
- Build a PFEP to enable you to analyze the full range of materials and develop the optimum supply chain and inventory settings for the materials involved in each value stream.
- Focus on reducing all three drivers of inventory—replenishment lead time, replenishment interval, and demand and supply variability.
- Build routine replenishment cycles where you aim to order the same products in the same quantities as frequently as possible.
- Work with suppliers and shippers to reduce lead time where possible. Remember that the actual transit times for freight are often only a

fraction of the total replenishment lead time. Therefore, there is usually lots of waste in the lead time that can be eliminated.

■ Regularly review your outsourced supply chain to ensure that you are still getting the best value in total cost terms. In recent years, the competitive landscape has changed, and it may be that the "low-cost supply" that you established several years ago is no longer truly low cost.

Case Study: Importing of Custom Sheet Metal Components from China to Australia

To understand the supply chain concepts in this chapter better, it is worth relating them to a case study. In this case, it was a project I worked on almost a decade ago that involved the outsourcing of the customized sheet metal components used by a major high-technology manufacturer in Australia. We had completed a formal bidding process and selected a supplier outside Shanghai to be the sole supplier for the 36 components shown in Table 8.3. The supply chain we established is shown in the value stream map in Figure 8.1.

The simple spreadsheet shown in Table 8.4 was all that was needed to control weekly ordering, *even though the Australian factory operated an advanced SAP ERP system.*

The ordering process was highly structured and routine. We had identified a regular weekly shipment from Shanghai to Melbourne that departed every Thursday, with the goods needing to be delivered to port every Tuesday. We agreed on a three-week lead time with the supplier, which was achievable due to the consistency of our demand. We then counted back three weeks and agreed with the supplier that we would place an order every Monday. Every Tuesday, the supplier would ship the goods we had ordered three weeks earlier. These goods would be delivered to the port of Shanghai to meet a ship that departed every Thursday. Every Thursday, the supplier would also provide an update on the status of all products on order that would be used to update the spreadsheet in Table 8.4.

To manage the shipping of the goods, we agreed on a contract with a third-party logistics provider who could offer us "door-to-door" service from the supplier's factory to the factory in Melbourne. The third-party logistics provider also warehoused the parts inventory at their warehouse in

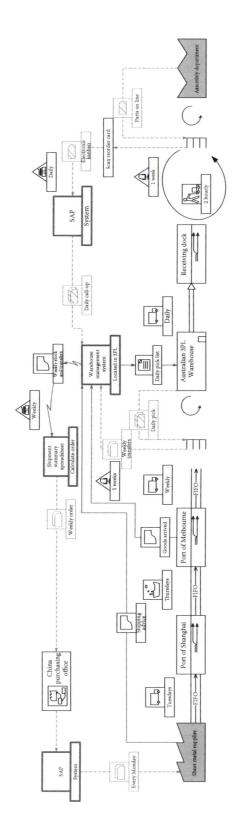

Figure 8.1 Value stream map of international supply chain highlighting the improvements put in place to reduce lead time, reduce inventory, and prevent shortages. 3PL, third-party logistics provider.

Melbourne. Our customer's factory in Melbourne then received daily deliveries from this warehouse and only held a small amount of stock in line side locations on the assembly line.*

Every Thursday, the third-party logistics provider also provided a weekly update of the stock on hand in their warehouse and shipments in transit, and this, combined with the inputs from the Chinese supplier, enabled the supply team at the factory to calculate the next order to be placed on the following Monday.

This supply chain delivered some dramatic improvements for the factory compared with earlier efforts to import parts from China. Lead times for imported parts were reduced from 16 weeks to 7 weeks. Inventory was reduced from around 16 weeks with frequent shortages and airfreight expediting to an average of 4 weeks with no parts shortages or airfreighting at all. The predictability of the demand for freight and shipping meant that the third-party logistics provider was able to negotiate overall transport rates 20% below those previously paid by the Melbourne factory. Finally, the original scope of the project envisaged four additional staff to manage the supply of parts in China and Australia and to expedite late deliveries. In the end, one person in Australia and one in China were able to comfortably manage this supply chain, including managing frequent new product introductions and product changes.

---

* The case study and value stream maps in Chapter 7 related to the same company, and therefore we had already streamlined the ordering and goods receiving process to reduce lead time and thus the inventory that needed to be held on site.

Chapter 9

Working with Suppliers

What You Will Learn in This Chapter

- *The reasons suppliers let you down*
- *The importance of putting yourself in your supplier's shoes*
- *Three basic rules for working with suppliers*
- *What a service level agreement is and how to develop one*
- *How to establish a firewall between you and your suppliers*
- *Developing long-term supplier relationships*
- *Establishing metrics to measure how you work with suppliers*
- *What to do when a supplier lets you down*

Are There Any Good Suppliers out There?

This question is one that I frequently hear from manufacturers and distributors around the world. It often seems an impossible task to find companies that will reliably and consistently supply your materials on time, in full, to your quality requirements, at a competitive price. Ask many companies with poor delivery performance what their number one cause of late deliveries is, and they will often point to shortages of materials. The cause of these shortages is, of course, poor supplier performance. Or is it?

In the earlier chapters, we discussed how a poorly designed supply chain, poor inventory management, and ineffective planning can lead to poor delivery performance. In Chapter 3, we discussed the challenges of trying to gain an accurate view of future demand through a forecast. Now put yourself in the shoes of your supplier (you can probably do this quite easily, as your business is likely to be a supplier to your customers). Your unstable supply chain is likely to lead to wild variations in your demand for materials. Your need for expediting to meet delivery deadlines is likely to generate constant schedule changes at the supplier. These changes are likely to require the supplier to deliver in a shorter lead time than their normal order fulfillment lead time. At the same time, your procurement team is probably driving hard for a lower price. It should be no surprise then that your supplier is likely to be finding it hard to meet your delivery requirements and will be bearing costs associated with providing you the level of service you need.

We typically see a vicious cycle emerge. Last-minute changes to your schedule and demand levels place demands on your suppliers that they cannot meet. As a result, you suffer shortages, which lead you to change your schedule and bring forward the production of products for which you have materials. This, however, then brings forward consumption of those materials, which leads to orders for them being triggered early and in greater quantities than your supplier expected. This causes further schedule changes at the supplier, which then are passed back up the supply chain to upstream processes and suppliers. As a result, the instability gets multiplied—your instability feeds instability in your supplier's process, which then feeds back more instability in your process. Your supplier simply cannot keep up with all the changes. This is a very common situation, and the result is that any form of regular planning with suppliers gets thrown out the window in favor of daily (and often hourly) discussions about priorities and changes to deliveries.

Understanding Your Supplier

The first step to achieving reliable and competitive supply is to listen to your suppliers. We are often very good at telling our suppliers what we want and how we want it. We are usually very ready to let them know when we have a problem or when we perceive them to have let us down. However, how often do we really listen to our suppliers? In my experience, most companies are more comfortable talking *about* their suppliers than they are talking *to* these suppliers.

Therefore, the first step to engaging your suppliers on your quest to achieve on-time, in-full delivery is to actually listen to them. The kind of things you might want to learn include

- What is the supplier's process for handling orders from your business?
- What problems does the supplier have working with you as a customer? Why do they think these problems occur?
- What sort of things can you do to help make things easier for your supplier?
- How much does your supplier know about your business, your demand patterns, and your future plans?
- Is the information you provide to the supplier adequate to enable them to plan effectively and meet your demand?
- What additional information does the supplier need in order for them to do a better job of delivering to your business in full and on time?
- Compared with their other customers, how important is your business to your supplier (i.e., approximately what proportion of their sales are to you as opposed to their other customers)?

You really need to put yourself in your suppliers' shoes and imagine what it would be like to be a supplier to your company. Given the constraints that the supplier has to work within and the information that you provide them, do you think your business could perform any better than your supplier currently does?

It can be really valuable to spend some time in their operation (even if it is overseas) and learn how your orders are processed through their system and products manufactured. This face-to-face contact can reveal many of the challenges and constraints that your supplier faces in a way that an e-mail or phone call cannot.

Some key information to learn from your supplier is

- What is their true order lead time (not the optimistic estimate provided to you by their salesperson in order to win your order)?
- Do they supply your business from inventory, or do they manufacture your products to order? Is this their preferred approach for your products and why?
- Does the manufacturing of your products require sourcing of special materials or parts that have long lead times or unreliable supply?

It can be good to create a simple current state value stream map of your suppliers' processes. Not every supplier will be open enough to allow you to gather this information, but with major suppliers, this can be invaluable, as it will reveal the whole end-to-end picture of their processes and highlight the problems and waste.

Basic Rules for Working with Suppliers

In working with suppliers, it is important to realize three essential rules:

1. It is not your business: As important as you might be to your supplier and as close as your integration with them may be, they are a separate business with separate ownership. Ultimately, the directors of your supplier's business have a legal obligation to make decisions in the interest of their own company, not yours. Unfortunately, I see too many buyers (especially from large companies) ignoring this fact and acting as if they "own" the supplier. This is a recipe for conflict and a poor relationship. No matter how "bad" you think the supplier is, it is up to them to change, not you. It is their business. Ultimately, if the supplier is not willing to improve, they are telling you that they no longer want or require your business and you should look elsewhere for supply.

2. Your supplier is trying to do a good job: When I was managing operations, I would often hear other managers complaining about the frontline workers. I would always argue that almost no one comes to work with the express purpose of doing a bad job. It is just the processes and culture that we as managers place them in that prevents them doing a good job. Exactly the same applies to your suppliers. They are invariably working hard to deliver a good product to you on time. It is failures of process and culture on both sides of the supply relationship (yours and theirs) that conspire to prevent this. As a result, the supplier will be on your side if you want to make things work more smoothly and efficiently and reduce problems.

3. You deserve good service and they deserve to be treated with respect: No matter how big your supplier is and how small your spend, you should expect to receive good service. This means that whatever you have agreed on with your supplier in terms of delivery lead times, quality, packaging, shipment procedures, and so forth, should be followed for every order. If not, you have a right to complain to your supplier (and should do so), and your supplier should be expected to remedy the immediate situation and put in place a permanent corrective action. On the other hand, you must also respect your supplier by first being courteous in your dealings with them, returning calls and e-mails, and responding to their requests promptly. Treating suppliers with respect also extends to not demanding unreasonable payment terms (in my view, payment terms longer than 30 days are unreasonable unless applied with very good reason), not

continually expecting supply in less than the agreed quantity or lead time, accepting responsibility for inventory held in good faith at your request, and avoiding spurious compensation claims or litigation.

I am now going to take you through some steps to building effective supplier relationships that will ensure that your suppliers can be effective partners in your quest to deliver on time, in full every time.

Be up Front from the Start

Many problems I see with suppliers originate with a lack of communication and thought at the start of the relationship. Often, the only detail clearly established is price, and the rest is just "made up as you go along." Introducing a new supplier can be quite exciting, and there is a tendency to overlook the details in order to get the first order underway. The supplier will also be pushing to "close the deal" so that they can start to see some of your money flowing into their bank account.

What do I mean by "from the start"? Ideally, the ground rules should be established even before the supplier has bid their prices. This way, the level of service and support you expect is "priced in" from the outset, removing a key basis for future conflict.

The outsourcing example I described in Chapter 8 involved outsourcing over $8 million in custom-made sheet metal parts to suppliers in China and Australia. For both the Chinese suppliers (described in Chapter 8) and the Australian suppliers, we developed detailed bid documents outlining our service expectations, including lead time, inventory held by the suppliers, prototyping procedures, delivery quantities, packaging requirements, and delivery frequency. Creating this took some time and thought, but meant that the successful suppliers knew exactly where they stood. The terms in the bid document were then built into the supply contract.

It is wise to take some time at the start of the new relationship, ideally before the first order is placed, to really understand each other's business and establish how your business relationship is going to work. Try to answer the key questions that I have outlined at the start of this chapter. Talk through (or ideally map out) the process for handling one of your orders from the generation of the demand at your end through the supplier's processes until the goods are delivered to your site. Be clear on the information flows—what you will provide to them, when, and in what format, and what they will provide to you, when, and in what format.

Establishing a Service Level Agreement

In establishing the rules of engagement with a new supplier up front, it is good to document this in a service level agreement. A service level agreement outlines the rules and procedures by which you plan to work with your new supplier. It is not necessarily a formal legal document and does not replace any formal contract you may have with a supplier. It acts essentially as "standard work" for the day-to-day operation of your relationship with your supplier. The type of things you might want to agree on in a service level agreement include:

- Procedures for ordering and supply of goods outlining who will do what, when, and how frequently
- Order lead times (these may vary from product to product)
- Standard order quantities
- Packaging requirements
- Maximum and minimum inventory to be held by the supplier, if any
- The process for introduction of new products and the obsolescence of old ones
- Key performance indicators measuring the supply relationship (these should involve measures on your performance, as well as your supplier's)
- Procedures for when things go wrong, including communication protocols and a requirement for root cause analysis and problem-solving, to prevent reoccurrence of problems

Putting in a Firewall

In most cases, at the outset of a supply relationship, or when you are a relatively small buyer, you may find your supplier reluctant to commit the time and trust necessary to open up their operation to you. It is also likely that your supplier's internal processes may not exactly suit the process you want to follow in your plant. For example, your supplier may like to run big batches that lead to long replenishment cycles and long lead times. You may see the opportunity to improve things, but your supplier may disagree or have other priorities. A simple answer in this situation might be to find another supplier. However, this may not always be possible. Therefore, an effective strategy to insulate your business from your supplier's internal processes is to put in what I call a "firewall" between yourself and your supplier.

This is a buffer of inventory or, in the case of make-to-order parts, lead time to insulate your business from your supplier's operation and you from theirs.

In the sheet metal outsourcing example that I describe above, our customer's in-house sheet metal department had successfully applied Lean over many years. As a result, the sheet metal shop could replenish parts to the assembly line in under four days. It was clear when we outsourced these parts that none of the potential local Australian suppliers could meet this lead time due to their processes of scheduling and their commitments to other customers. On the other hand, we did not want to increase the amount of inventory held in our customer's factory. The solution therefore was to put an inventory firewall between the suppliers and our customer. This meant that for the majority of parts, the supplier was required to carry a minimum of two Kanbans and a maximum of six Kanbans worth of inventory. By setting the minimum at two Kanbans instead of one, we ensured that if for any reason our customer pulled the same part number twice in the same week, a shortage would not occur. The maximum stock level, on the other hand, was set to prevent the supplier manufacturing excessively large batches and creating obsolete stock when a design change occurred. For low-volume parts, we provided a different form of buffer. For these parts, we ensured that the reorder point represented at least six weeks' inventory. As a result, the supplier would supply these on a make-to-order basis and our customer would hold sufficient stock to enable the supplier to achieve this without having a shortage. The requirement to hold this inventory was included in the bid process, and then the procedure written into a service level agreement.

Relationships That Go beyond the Purchase Order

One of the good things about a service level agreement is that it assumes that your relationship with the supplier will be ongoing. Surprisingly, I find that many companies have no formal documented relationships with their suppliers. This can even occur with suppliers who may be key to the business and with whom the company may have been dealing for many years. In these situations, I like to tell the companies that their relationship with their supplier will end with the fulfillment of the current purchase order. Of course, they scoff at this suggestion, pointing to the fact that they have been buying off that supplier for years and that they have a great relationship "based on a handshake." When I talk to these suppliers, I usually get a different response. When you have no formal agreement with a supplier and provide no forecast of your expected requirements, your supplier is entitled to assume that your current purchase order will be the last one you place with them. The supplier, if they are wise, will not assume that you will buy from them this month just because you purchased from them last month. As a result, the supplier will be reluctant to purchase materials needed to manufacture your products, allocate production capacity, or invest in people or machines to make your product. When a new customer comes along, the supplier is perfectly entitled to switch their capacity to meeting that customer's needs because they have no assurance of whether you will ever order off them again.

It is therefore important to establish some form of supply agreement with your key suppliers. This does not need to be a 50-page legal tome and does not need to commit you to purchasing any particular volume of products or to source those products exclusively from the supplier. They can often be not much more than a price list, a high-level monthly forecast, and/or a service level agreement, and may not involve legal documents at all. The important thing is that the supplier clearly knows your intention (everything going well) to keep purchasing from them for a period into the future. This enables them to plan their operations with some confidence that your business will be ongoing. Commercially, most suppliers will "pay" for this type of security, so a 12-month or longer contract, even if it offers no firm commitment to volumes, will usually allow a supplier to offer the goods they supply you at a lower price.

Importance of Metrics

Once we have set things up with our supplier, established a clear service agreement, and placed our first order, everything should go smoothly. This sounds nice in theory, but the reality is that without vigorous monitoring, procedures will soon deviate from the standard procedure. As a result, your service level agreement should establish some metrics to measure the performance of your supply chain. These metrics will vary from business to business, but typical metrics on your supplier might include

- Supplier on-time, in-full delivery: This mirrors your own measure and is the number of orders delivered to you on the agreed date and in the quantity required compared with the total number of orders received.
- Delivery within agreed lead time and in full: A variation to measuring on time, in full is to measure your supplier's performance against the lead time agreed on in your service level agreement. When your business expedites product in shorter than the standard lead time, it is reasonable to expect that there is increased risk the supplier will deliver late.
- Actual lead time achieved: This becomes a measure of how your supply chain is functioning. If your supplier has committed to a 7-day lead time, but is actually achieving an average of 10 days, then the root causes of lateness need to be addressed or the standard lead time needs to be increased to reflect reality. Alternatively, if the supplier consistently delivers early, this might present an opportunity to reduce the standard lead time, enabling you to reduce inventory.
- Inventory on hand by part number: This is a measure of how much inventory the supplier is holding on your behalf and is a good check that the supplier is ensuring that enough inventory is in place to prevent shortages, while at the same time excessive inventory is not being built up, creating a risk of obsolescence.
- Number of quality complaints, product returns, quality credits, or defective products: There are a lot of metrics that can be used to measure quality. Choose one or two that are easy to measure and make sense for your business.
- Internal defect or rework rates: If your supplier is prepared to share their internal rate of defects or rework associated with the manufacture of your product, this can be a good leading indicator of the quality you are likely to receive. Unfortunately, many companies do not measure this, and many of those who do may be unwilling to share it, but it is worth asking.

On your side, there are some measures that show how you are complying with your agreements with your supplier.

- Number of orders placed with less than the agreed lead time relative to total orders placed: This will show whether instability in your process is impacting your supplier.

◼ Monthly forecast accuracy: This is as simple as total volume purchased by value stream compared with forecast volume. This is an indicator for how well you are predicting your high-level demand. This information can be as important for the supplier's sales and operation planning process as it is for yours.*

There are a lot of other metrics that you can measure, and I will leave it up to you to decide exactly what you choose. However, for major suppliers of key products, I recommend that you share a monthly report with your suppliers. With many ERP systems, these reports can be automated, saving a lot of work (assuming the information is accurate).

Managing Poor-Performing Suppliers

So far, I have painted a fairly optimistic view of suppliers. You might be led to thinking that achieving reliable on-time, in-full quality supply is as simple as getting your own house in order and having a good service level agreement. Unfortunately, it is not that simple.

In reality, you will be let down by suppliers. In particular, unless you are starting a completely green fields operation, you will have legacy issues in supply relationships that may go back many years. Poor performance may have gone unchallenged and costly work-arounds developed. Past conflicts with suppliers may have left a legacy of ill will and mistrust on both sides. Your business may have grown in scale and sophistication so that your historical suppliers are no longer able to meet your needs. There are any number of reasons why you can have genuine problems with suppliers beyond those caused by the poor operation of your own supply chain.

The challenge is how you manage these problems. The first step, as I outlined earlier in the chapter, is to sit down and talk to the supplier. Listen to their issues and try to understand their perspective. Don't bully or lecture them. Using a formal problem-solving process such as A3 problem-solving[†]

---

* My frequent references to forecasts in this chapter do not contradict my thoughts on forecasts expressed in Chapter 3. The forecast you need to provide your supplier is a high-level rolling monthly forecast of your demand, not a detailed, week-by-week, item-by-item forecast. The detailed forecast might look impressive, but its inaccuracy will just confuse your suppliers. The high-level monthly forecast will enable them to plan their capacity and resources through their sales and operations planning process.

† A3 problem-solving is the analysis of a problem using the plan–do–check–method using a template on a single A3 sheet of paper.

can help you and your supplier examine the problem in a rational and dispassionate way and find the root causes of problems. As I have suggested, supply problems are rarely all the supplier's fault, and insisting that this is the case will rarely lead to a mutually agreed resolution with your supplier.

Beyond this, you need to protect your business. There are a number of strategies for this. Inventory buffers can assist to provide time for you and your supplier to sort out issues or for you to source another supplier. However, be careful when deciding to build up inventory. If you hit your poor-performing supplier with a large amount of additional orders to build stock, you may make the problem worse by overloading their operations.

Another important strategy is to have a backup supplier. Things go wrong in the best supplier relationships, so where possible, it makes sense to have two approved suppliers for each key product that you buy. This is particularly the case when your supplier is supplying you from a single facility. As much as you would not wish a fire or natural disaster on your supplier, you don't want such an event to wipe out your business as well. The challenge with dual sourcing is getting the balance right between the two suppliers. If your backup supplier sees too little business, they may not have the capacity or the interest to ramp up when you need them. Alternatively, if you split the business evenly, you may find that neither supplier gets enough volume to make your business truly interesting to them.

You also need to resist the temptation to use dual sourcing purely as a price lever. Any supplier contract will likely have an end date, and at the end of that period, it is wise to offer the opportunity to other suppliers to bid on the business, in order to ensure that the prices you are using are competitive. However, I have seen companies play their suppliers off against each other from one order to the next. This is not a good way to build a positive supplier relationship, and ultimately, it will not lead to lower prices, as suppliers eventually refuse to play your game and you get faced with "take it or leave it" pricing. Some of the large automotive original equipment manufacturers (OEMs) have engaged in this kind of aggressive price arbitrage over many years with the result that many suppliers have diversified away from automotive business and put themselves in a position where they can tell the automotive OEMs "where to go" on price. This type of aggressive commercial approach also does not lead to good collaboration on improving the supply chain (or on innovation for that matter).

An effective dual-sourcing arrangement means that both suppliers have a long-term relationship with you, understand the rules of engagement, and have a reasonable understanding of what business to expect from you and at what price.

Another key problem with dual sourcing is that the same product delivered from two different suppliers is never completely the same. Therefore, it makes sense to dedicate certain part numbers to particular suppliers.

In the sheet metal sourcing project mentioned above, we selected two Australian suppliers with approximately equal shares of the business. The work was allocated to each supplier in packs of parts associated with each finished goods assembly; however, the nature of the parts in each pack was similar. When one of the suppliers ran into financial difficulty and could not supply, we were able to quickly transfer their work packs to the other supplier and suffered minimum interruption to supply.

Summary

As I think you will gather from above, there is no easy solution when a supplier runs off the rails. Without a doubt, the best strategy is to avoid this situation occurring in the first place. Achieving this requires

- A clear understanding of what you require from your supplier, in regard to both the details of the products to be supplied and the operation of the supply chain
- Ensuring that those requirements are clearly communicated to the supplier, ideally in writing through a service level agreement
- Maintaining open lines of communication with your suppliers and listening to what they have to say when problems occur (and even when problems are not occurring)
- Measuring suppliers' performance in supplying you, as well as your performance in working with suppliers regularly and ensuring problems found are acted on in a collaborative way
- Keeping an eye on supply chain risk and not leaving your business overly exposed to unexpected events

If you are careful in selecting suppliers, treat them with respect, and work collaboratively and openly, you are likely to find them an asset in your quest to deliver quality products to customers on time and in full every time.

Chapter 10

Making the Best Use of Your ERP System

What You Will Learn in This Chapter

- *The functions and benefits of an ERP system*
- *The limitations of an ERP system and why MRP replenishment causes so many problems*
- *How to get the most out of your ERP*
- *Selecting the right ERP system for your business*
- *Key tips to successfully implementing an ERP system*

In the last nine chapters, I have frequently referred to a software tool called an enterprise resource planning (ERP) system. I have highlighted many problems with the use of these systems. Many of you might now be wondering what to do with that big investment you made in your ERP software. Alternatively, you may be frustrated with trying to run your business on Excel spreadsheets and wondering if an ERP is not the solution to your problems, what is? Therefore, in this chapter I am going to talk about what ERP systems do, how to use them effectively, and why you will probably need one in some point in your business's life cycle.

What Is an ERP System?

An ERP system is a software product. There are literally hundreds on the market, and they vary enormously in scale, complexity, capabilities, and cost. Essentially, an ERP system is intended to record and control the complete day-to-day operations of a business, from taking an order to shipping finished goods to everything in between. The more advanced packages can incorporate additional functions, such as cost estimating, payroll, forecasting, maintenance management, warehouse location management, and highly advanced scheduling tools. Most importantly, a good ERP system is also the business's accounting system. This means that day-to-day transactions such as receiving goods, raising purchase orders, completing production, and making a sale are recorded directly into the accounting general ledger. This avoids the need for double entry of data and provides the accounting team with (hopefully) an accurate and direct insight into the operations of the business, which they can in turn use to provide accurate information and reports to management for decision-making. For example, if operated correctly, the ERP system will provide an accurate calculation of the value of inventory in the business, rather than requiring the inventory to be physically counted every time the accounting team need to update the balance sheet.

The ERP system can also automate tasks, saving time and reducing double entry. For example, a sales order can be automatically allocated to a production order. The system can then record the creation of finished goods inventory and consumption of material and work-in-progress inventory when the production order is completed (this process is called "back flushing"). This saves a lot of time because rather than recording these transactions on a separate system or spreadsheet and then manually entering them into the company's accounting system, the ERP will complete this transaction automatically.

Another key value of an ERP system is to enable you to track the costs of doing business. This is difficult to do manually, but a well-set-up ERP system with accurate costs, routings, bills of materials, and good systems for labor recording can do it with ease. One of the most important ways to improve business performance is to understand which product lines make money for the business and which do not. This is particularly essential in a jobbing environment where the ability to quote a job and deliver it within the quoted amount is critical to the survival and success of the business. Working this out accurately is often easier said than done, but it is ideally suited for an ERP system.

As a business grows, its number of customers and numbers of products increase, and therefore the number of transactions occurring every day can increase exponentially. The right time to implement an ERP system will vary from business to business. However, I have seen very few manufacturing and distribution businesses turning over more than $5 million per year who were operating effectively *without* an ERP system in place. A good ERP system that is fit for your business's purpose and that has been deployed with care and thoroughness will be a huge benefit.

So What Is the Problem with ERP Systems?

I have something of a reputation as an ERP skeptic and have written on many occasions about the problems with using ERP systems, including earlier in this book. Nevertheless, you have just read an endorsement of ERP systems and a claim that most manufacturing and distribution businesses will need an ERP system at some point in their growth. So how can I reconcile these apparently opposing views of the same software tool?

The issue is how you use the ERP system and what you use it for. ERP systems offer a lot, and most leaders in business love technology. Therefore, the temptation most succumb to is to try to get the ERP to run the whole business "at the push of a button."

At the core of the problem is the use of material requirements planning (MRP), which is one part of the ERP system. What the MRP does is calculate your requirements for finished goods, work in progress, and materials. It essentially tells you what to make, when to make it, what materials to order, and when to order them. To do this, it uses a forecast (remember Chapter 3). The ERP contains a big table of business rules and data called the master production schedule (MPS). This includes things like lead times for key processes and supplies, safety stock levels, optimum production and order quantities, and rules about how and when to schedule production. With advanced planning and optimization systems, this will go all the way down to scheduling the sequence of work on individual work centers and doing "finite scheduling" where demand is allocated to manage production capacity.

The MRP is a big calculator, working its way through thousands of transactions. Typically, it will run every night, but often, businesses will only run MRP weekly. When a forecast for finished goods is entered into the ERP system, MRP will then calculate the impact of that updated forecast. The forecast will show requirements for the supply of finished goods into the future. The MRP will start at these future dates and work back. First, it will look at the MPS data and identify the safety stock for each item. It will work into the future progressively deducting the forecast sales off the inventory until the point where the inventory falls below the safety stock. It will then schedule a production run for that, allowing for the production lead time (that has been input in the MPS) to ensure that the goods are manufactured in time to replenish the finished goods inventory before the inventory runs out. Once the MRP has scheduled the production, it will then look at the routing of the product and allocate the production to the work centers specified in the routing, and may also allocate labor, tooling, and other resources. The MRP then looks at the bill of materials for the product it has just scheduled and calculates the quantity of materials needed to manufacture those products. This might include creating new production orders to make work-in-progress items, but will ultimately end up with demand for materials. It will aggregate this demand and then produce purchase suggestions for the purchase of the materials needed for the scheduled production. Again, it will work back in time based on the lead times set in the MPS to ensure that it orders materials sufficiently early to ensure that they arrive in time for the scheduled production. Sometimes, raw material safety stock may be set, but often, raw materials are ordered to match the future demand (with a small allowance for waste). If it all works well, the raw materials will arrive in time for production, work in progress will be manufactured in time for use in final assembly, and then the finished goods will replenish the shelves to keep up with customer demand.

It is easy to see how such a sophisticated, logical, and automated process could inspire such faith. However, in my view, the MRP system has some fundamental flaws that mean it is often not the most effective way to ensure that your business delivers on time, in full to customers at a competitive cost.

First, if you refer back to Chapter 3, the whole MRP is built on the assumption that the forecast is accurate (or at least reasonably accurate). However, for the reasons outlined in Chapter 3, forecasts are inevitably not accurate. Over the years, I have heard many business managers and supply chain managers bemoaning the inability of their customers and sales teams to provide an accurate forecast. Some will go as far as actually penalizing customers with longer lead times and poor service if they provide inaccurate forecasts. This sounds like a very good reason for your customers to look elsewhere. Without accurate forecasts, the whole MRP model falls down, as the system ends up making and ordering the wrong stuff in the wrong quantities at the wrong time. Schedulers and buyers then spend their days frantically expediting the materials and production actually needed to meet real customer demand. It is just so much simpler to instead adopt a pull system where products and materials are replenished as they are used based on *actual* demand, not a forecast.

Second, the ERP system requires the data in the system to be completely accurate all the time. "Master data," such as bills of materials, routings, and lead times, need to be kept up to date and accurate at all times. In particular, inventory levels in the system need to match actual inventory with a high degree of accuracy. This would seem simple, but is hard to do in real time. This is because there are usually delays between the actual transaction occurring and it being recorded in the system. Therefore, the ERP system will often calculate based on the assumption that inventory exists when it has already been used.

For example, a company we worked with manufactured a complex assembly. The daily output was six machines, and the lead time to manufacture was two days. Therefore, at any one time up to 12 machines were in production. Completion of the production order and back flushing of the parts consumed did not occur until after the product had passed its final test of the product and been received into the warehouse. This was usually a day later. Therefore, up to three days of parts would be recorded as being available on the shelf when in fact they had already been used in the manufacture of incomplete products.

Supply chain experts reading this will say that it is simply a matter of discipline and suggest that "real-time" production recording systems, such as barcode scanning, can overcome these issues. This is true, but it takes a considerable effort to keep all the data needed for correct MRP functioning accurate all the time. It seems a wasted effort when simpler, more robust systems for scheduling and replenishment exist, such as Lean level production, first-in, first-out (FIFO) lanes, and pull systems.

Finally, a flaw in the operation of the MRP system can actually make the problem of supply chain variation worse. This is called the bullwhip effect or Forrester effect. It is best illustrated by an example.

Many years ago, I managed a packaging factory that was supplying bottles for Australia's leading brand of dish washing liquid. This customer was perhaps our most difficult to service. Every week, we received a forecast update that usually presented us with a wide range of dramatic changes from the previous week. Production we had already made was no longer required, while items that we had not even scheduled were suddenly required for urgent delivery. This customer had an experienced supply chain team and a modern ERP system. What was strange about all this volatility was that consumer demand for dish washing liquid is almost completely constant all year. Occasionally, the product would be promoted, but overall, the end consumer demand was predictable (if gradually falling due to the growth of automatic dishwashers). What was causing all this volatility was the bullwhip effect.

The bullwhip effect is caused by forecast error combined with batching of demand. Essentially, what happens is that the sale of one bottle of dish washing liquid might trigger the opening of a new box full of bottles. Therefore, the actual use of 1 bottle can lead to the replenishment of 12 bottles in the supermarket. However, the usage of one box may trigger the opening of another pallet in the warehouse, so that sale of one bottle of dish washing liquid has now triggered replenishment of a pallet of 192 bottles. This pallet of bottles now takes the customer's warehouse below safety stock so that it now triggers ordering of a minimum order of five pallets or 960 bottles. This order is now recorded in the sales history of the supplier as demand for 960 bottles. Forecasts are generally built from sales history, and so this demand spike for 960 bottles is built into the forecast. The MRP then generates purchase requirements to trigger the replenishment of materials based on the forecast. By the time this demand gets to the packaging supplier, it is just as likely to trigger a new production run of thousands of bottles. This can all be triggered by one person buying one bottle of dish washing liquid in one supermarket!

Making the volatility worse in this case was the fact that the supplier was using "dynamic safety stock" that adjusted the level of safety stock automatically, depending on forecast demand. This had the effect of further amplifying the variation. Their ERP system was likely to misinterpret an artificial spike in demand caused by the bullwhip effect for a real increase in demand. It would therefore increase safety stock, bringing forward orders and production requirements. Then, once the demand spike had passed, dynamic safety stock promptly decreased safety stock, pushing those same requirements out into the future.

By contrast, Lean "pull" replenishment tends to damp out the Forrester effect, by just replenishing the material that has been consumed, after it has been consumed, and no more.

All this means that the MRP functionality of the ERP system should definitely be "handled with care," if it is to be used at all. Some companies like to use it for low-usage long-lead-time items, but I find this illogical, as it is these materials where the forecast replenishment model works the worst.

One company I worked with used MRP replenishment for low-usage long-lead-time items (and Kanban for more common items). It was easy to tell the MRP items on the shelves, as they were the ones where the part bins were always filled to overflowing and excess stock was stored in the warehouse.

In my view, you are better off not using the MRP function at all and instead using the Lean scheduling and replenishment systems that I recommend in this book. However, this does not mean that an ERP system may not be a useful addition to your business. So if you are not using the MRP, what are you going to need an ERP for?

The Right Time to Purchase an ERP System

At some point in your growth, you will find that the sheer volume of transactions is more than your old spreadsheet-based systems and a simple accounting package can cope with. Typically, you will be finding it impossible to keep track of inventory despite large amounts of staff time constantly counting stock and updating spreadsheets, you may have difficulty knowing the costs of your products, and your accounting team will spend much of their time in data entry. At this point, you will start thinking about a software solution to your problems.

Selecting an ERP System

There is a bewildering array of ERP systems on the market, from global names like SAP and Oracle to small providers who may only operate in one city. So how do you select the right ones for your business? Here are some points to consider:

1. Be clear on what you want the ERP to do. This means mapping your key business and financial processes, ideally using value stream maps or swim lane charts (Figure 10.1). By mapping your processes, you are in a position to tell the ERP provider exactly what you want the system to do and ensuring that their proposed system provides the capabilities you need.
2. Consider whether you want the ERP to do everything or whether you want to integrate the ERP system with other specialized software packages. Many ERP systems will offer a full range of functions, including demand management, warehouse management, timekeeping, maintenance management, and customer relationship management. However, often specialized software packages in these areas will be cheaper and more effective than the ERP module. This may mean that you achieve a

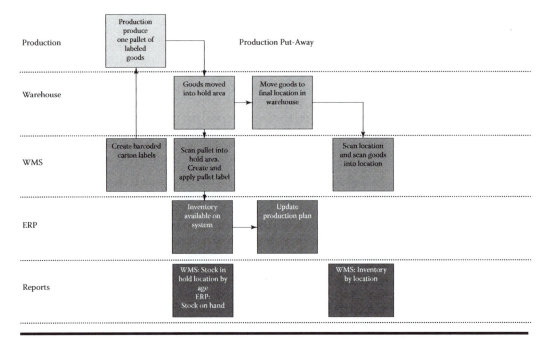

Figure 10.1   Swim lane chart for the process of receiving and putting away stock. In this case, the chart maps the interaction between the ERP and a warehouse management system (WMS). The swim lane chart shows the movement of information between systems and functions.

better outcome by purchasing a simpler ERP, provided it has good interfacing tools for these other packages, rather than buying a big expensive ERP that tries to do everything.

3. Consider the information you want to get out of the system. Some ERP systems have very limited reporting functionality and very high costs when you want to write custom reports. On the other hand, many ERP systems enable you to write reports in a database package such as Microsoft Access that directly queries the ERP database. This is a great feature, as it enables you to get exactly the data you need for your business.

4. Consider an industry-specific solution. There are many ERP packages designed for specific industries. This can often (but not always) be helpful. For example, I have come across packages specifically designed for printing, joinery, and engineering jobbing shops.

5. Do not just consider one package. Do a thorough evaluation of at least three packages so that you learn about the differences in functions and performance. Even if you end up with the package you originally

intended to go with, considering the others will help you understand exactly why it is a good fit, and also perhaps raise some questions for the software vendor that may assist in your choice.

6. Get references. It is essential that you actually talk to people already using the package. Ideally, go and see the reference site and talk to people using the system. Do not just talk to the information technology (IT) manager or supply chain manager, who may have been the internal advocates of the package (and so have to defend their decision), but talk to the actual users—people like customer service operators, warehouse clerks, and production schedulers. Go armed with specific questions about the functions you need the ERP to perform, and try to confirm that the proposed solution can actually do these things (if you can).

7. Be sure about the level of support that will be offered for your chosen package. This is the number one complaint I hear about ERP systems, the lack of support for implementation and ongoing operation. Do not assume that the big-name packages will be any better on this. Many of them sell their products through third-party resellers, and it is the reseller that you will be buying support from. You need to be clear that they will be there when you need them. In fact, after-sales support is the reason why many smaller local or regional solution providers can be a good option, as they tend to be more committed to providing high-quality support in their market area.

8. Recognize that the most expensive solution is not necessarily the best. I have often see companies purchase big-name ERP systems because they assume that the famous name will give them better functionality, better performance, and better support. While I am not saying that you should not buy the big-name package, in reality, high price should not be a positive selection criterion. I suggest looking at the seven points above, and if the big famous provider comes out as the best option, then consider them.

Successfully Implementing Your ERP

Even after the best planning in the selection process, often, implementing an ERP system can be a very difficult venture. When it goes wrong, an ERP implementation can cause incredible levels of stress on you and your staff, directly impact the quality of service you deliver to customers, and totally distract your team from all the other issues and opportunities facing the business.

So how do you avoid a "train wreck" implementation? The answer starts with some project management basics. These apply to any project, not just ERP implementation. My rules for good project management are pretty simple.

1. Start by deciding how you will resource the project. An ERP project is a major venture, and it needs dedicated resources. It cannot just be added to the list of things to do for busy managers. Ideally, you need to release people to focus solely on the project and backfill their normal roles so that they are not distracted. As well, you should consider what other projects are in progress and decide whether these can proceed in parallel with the ERP implementation. Be conservative—it is better to delay the ERP rollout or some of the other projects rather than take on too much. If you try to do them all at once and find you cannot cope, it is likely to impact *all* the projects, as well as your ongoing business.

2. Set up a project governance structure. This means having an ERP implementation team that would meet weekly or even have a daily "stand-up" meeting. This team would include the key operational people closest to the ERP project and may include representatives of the software company. As well as the implementation team, you will need a steering committee. This includes the senior representatives of the implementation team, along with the most senior managers impacted directly or indirectly by the implementation. For example, in a manufacturing business, the steering committee would need to include the general manager or CEO, sales manager, manufacturing manager, supply chain manager, IT manager, finance manager, and ERP project manager. This group would meet less frequently (perhaps monthly). It would have responsibility for overviewing the project progress, ensuring the project has sufficient resources, ensuring that all the relevant stakeholders are engaged, and making key decisions at milestones, such as the "go-live" date.

3. Make sure you have a detailed project schedule and budget. The ERP provider will often put together a project schedule using Microsoft Project or a similar tool. This is great if they provide you that, but make sure that your project team integrates this into their own schedule, rather than just relying on the software vendor.

Once you have set up your project management structure, there are some key areas you need to focus on to ensure you project is successful.

Ensure You Have Accurate Master Data

This includes ensuring that bills of materials, product routings, customer data, pricing, product descriptions and data, supplier data, and so forth, are 100% accurate. There needs to be a very thorough process of checking and validating this data. The ERP system relies on this data and will make many automated decisions based on it. Therefore, if it is wrong, you will find that your deliveries are going to the wrong customer address, you will be ordering the wrong materials, from the wrong supplier, and you will be making any number of other mistakes at a time when you are already busy trying to get used to using the new system.

A common assumption is that you can just output all the data from your legacy systems and upload it into the new systems. I recommend that you do not do this without a thorough line-by-line checking of all this data. Otherwise, all the errors and omissions in your legacy system will be uploaded into the new system. The new system is likely to be more interconnected, and so it will be less tolerant of incorrect data and the consequences of this data will be more severe.

I was involved in the "postmortem" after the New Zealand division of a major packaging company implemented a large ERP system several years ago. Unfortunately, the senior management did not fully engage in the project and the review of master data was cursory, to say the least. As a result, a large proportion of the bills of materials, routings, customer files, and supplier files imported into the new ERP system were incorrect, incomplete, or both. The consequence was that this company's on-time, in-full delivery went from 98% to 0% (yes, you read that right); they stopped production at New Zealand's largest brewery and permanently lost around 10% of their customers. So, it pays to take time over your master data!

Keep Bill of Material Structures and Routings Simple

When your process has multiple steps, you may be tempted to have what are called multilevel bills of materials. This means that the final assembly is made from a number of work-in-progress part numbers. Each work-in-progress part number then has its own routing and bill of materials made up of perhaps raw materials and lower-level subassemblies. In turn, these "third-level" subassemblies may be made from fourth-level subassemblies, which have their own part numbers, bills of materials, and routings. In theory, multilevel bills of materials accurately reflect your process. You do actually make inventory of work-in-progress parts at each stage of the process. In reality, however, multilevel bills of material can be a nightmare. The dynamic nature of production means that often, by the time a subassembly is recorded at one level in production, it has already been converted into the next stage in the process. This leads to wildly inaccurate inventory and, when the MRP runs, incorrect recommendations to replenish subassemblies. I worked with one company whose bills of materials had up to eight levels, and this led to massive problems with shortages of subassemblies, as well as overproduction. My preferred solution combines Lean thinking with ERP thinking:

1. Reduce your end-to-end process lead time as far as you can with Lean process design—use a value stream map as described in Chapter 2.
2. Design as few layers to your bill of materials as you can. Ideally, aim for single-level bills of materials with just materials and finished goods.
3. Control work in progress using visual lean systems such as Kanban and FIFO lanes. This will ensure that work in progress is controlled within a fixed range. Since the lead time will be short, the work-in-progress value will be low and you can manage it with an allowance in your balance sheet that is validated by periodic stock counts.
4. Replenish materials using a Kanban pull system, as described earlier in Chapter 7, so that the delay in completing an order and back flushing the materials from your inventory file does not affect replenishment. Using barcodes to track issuing and consumption of materials can also aid in this, as can issuing materials in kits from a central warehouse (although this last process does add some waste to your process).
5. Avoid alternate materials, and if you use them, ensure that you have strict processes to manage their use. Many businesses will allow materials from different suppliers to be used as alternates in a bill of materials. That means if you are out of stock of the item from one supplier, you can just use the material from the other supplier. Alternate materials are very rarely exactly the same, and therefore you increase the risk of defects and quality problems. From an ERP perspective, alternate materials create a high risk of inventory errors. There has to be a very high level of discipline to make sure that the use of the alternate material is recorded. Otherwise, when the finished goods are received and the inventory back flushed, the ERP system will record consumption against the wrong material and you will create an inventory error for both the alternate and the preferred material. If alternate materials are

used frequently, this can create a huge number of inventory variances very quickly.

Be Flexible about the Go-Live Date

Often, go-live dates for software launches get cast in stone and the whole business drives toward that date. A lot of management ego can get tied up in delivering the project on time. This is important, but often, things disrupt the schedule or the implementation turns out to be more complex than expected. Ensuring ongoing supply to customers is more important to your business than launching your ERP on a particular date. Therefore, if your steering committee believes the business is not ready to switch over to the new system, then be prepared to delay the go-live date.

Focus Training and Support after Go-Live

Some training is necessary for key frontline staff before you go live. This should include "war-gaming" key activities and transactions to make sure that the system can do what is required when it starts up. For example, I have seen implementations where the business has discovered after go-live that the process of entering a customer order takes three times as long as it did with the old legacy system. In a busy customer service office, this can be catastrophic. Therefore, it pays to test out these key transactions beforehand so that these problems can be ironed out. Beyond that, most companies spend too much money and time on training before going live. Usually, the information goes in one ear and out the other. It is only when someone has to enter a real order for a real customer or create a real purchase order on a real supplier that he or she actually really learns how to use the system and finds the gaps in his or her knowledge. That is the time when plenty of expert resources need to be available to answer queries and provide coaching promptly to ensure the business keeps running and mistakes are minimized.

Summary

As your business grows, you will need to improve the systems you employ in order to manage the rapidly increased number of transactions occurring.

Therefore, an ERP system that provides a direct connection between the day-to-day operational transactions of a business and its finance system will be a necessary investment. However, poor implementation and/or overreliance on MRP functionality within an ERP system can lead to poor on-time delivery performance, high inventory, and high costs. To gain the benefits of an ERP system while ensuring you maintain high levels of on-time delivery at minimum inventory, we recommend the following approach:

■ Design and implement your Lean fulfillment systems first, as I have described in Chapters 2 through 8. From my experience, these are simpler to operate, more reliable, and will deliver better outcomes than forecast-based MRP fulfillment.

■ By clearly defining your business processes first, you will be much clearer on what you need out of your ERP system and more likely to select the software system you need rather than what the software salesperson wants to sell you.

■ Consider buying a simpler ERP system and then interfacing specialist tools for warehouse management, maintenance management, and so forth. These tools are often cheaper and more capable than the comparable ERP "modules."

■ Apply careful due diligence in selecting your ERP system, including developing a clearly defined specification, evaluating multiple vendors, and checking reference sites.

■ Implementing an ERP is a big complex project, and it is *not* acceptable to tell customers that you "can't deliver because you have a new system." Therefore, thorough project planning is needed to ensure that you have the right resources, governance structure, and a credible project schedule for the implementation.

■ Beyond general good project management practice, a successful ERP implementation requires accurate master data, accurate inventory records, accurate assumptions about your process, flexibility around your go-live dates, and support for frontline staff to adapt to the new system—especially after you go live.

■ In designing the ERP system, avoid overly complicated bill of material and routing structures and use of alternate materials, as these can make management of materials extremely hard, if not impossible.

Chapter 11

Managing a Distribution Network

What You Will Learn in This Chapter

- *What a distribution network is and why you need one*
- *Why distribution networks fail to deliver on time and in full to customers, despite high levels of inventory*
- *The factors to consider when designing your distribution network*

So far, we have only talked about achieving operation from a single factory and warehouse. But what if you distribute your products through a network of branch stores, warehouses, or retail stores?* How do you achieve on-time, in-full delivery then?

Many businesses face this challenge, with some servicing clients through dozens of local branch stores across a wide geographic area. Many of the principles outlined so far apply at the branch store level; however, the relationship between branch stores and central warehouses (distribution centers) adds an additional level of complexity that is essential to understand and manage if you are to achieve on-time, in-full delivery from the branch stores.

---

* Downstream distribution points in a distribution network are variously referred to as warehouses, branch stores, or stores. For the sake of simplicity in this book, I use the term *branch store*. Likewise, I refer to the upstream warehouses that supply goods to the branch stores as distribution centers for both retailing and wholesaling.

Why Do You Need a Distribution Network?

Businesses usually operate distribution networks to provide local service to customers. There may be several reasons for this. In retail and some industrial products categories, the business may benefit from significant "walk-in" sales where customers physically visit branch stores to purchase the goods they need off the shelf. Clearly in this case, having branch stores located in places that are easily accessible to large numbers of potential customers is an advantage. Retailers carry out detailed demographic research and put considerable effort into finding the right branch store locations. In industrial products distribution or wholesaling, walk-in shoppers are less likely to be important, as goods are likely to be delivered to the site. In this case, the benefits of having a local branch store are usually quick service and the availability of sales and technical support. In a large country such as Australia, a local branch store can also perform a cross-docking function where freight savings are achieved by delivering large, consolidated loads to the branch store, which are then broken up into smaller loads for distribution to customers. It is important that you clearly understand the reasons why you have your branch store network, whatever they are, because operating a distribution network usually adds significant cost to your business when compared with distributing all your goods from a single point. Every branch you add will increase overheads in the form of management staff, rent, and insurances and will require additional inventory.

Key Elements of a Distribution Network

Most distribution networks operate a "hub and spoke" model. This means that suppliers deliver goods to one or more "hub" locations or distribution centers, and then these distribution centers distribute the goods to the "spoke" locations, which then sell the goods to the customers. Variations on this exist; for example, the hub distribution center may also operate as a spoke branch store for its local area. The hub distribution center may also offer direct deliveries to large customers outside its area. This can avoid the cost of handling the goods in a spoke branch. Sometimes, there may be three levels of distribution, with a central distribution center supplying regional distribution centers, which then supply branch stores.

Apart from the distribution centers and branch stores themselves, you also need a method of deciding when and how to replenish the branch stores and distribution centers, and how much inventory to hold. This means that you need some form of system for replenishment and inventory management to ensure that you have the right goods in the right place in the right quantity at the right time.

Finally, you need to determine how you will move goods through your distribution network from suppliers to the distribution centers, from the distribution centers to the branch stores, and then from the branch stores to the customer. Therefore, your distribution network needs a transportation system.

Unfortunately, in many distribution networks these key elements of network design, replenishment, inventory management systems, and transportation systems are *ad hoc* and not properly defined. Poor and inconsistent definitions of these distribution network elements can be a root cause of poor on-time, in-full delivery, as well as being a cause of high inventory and costs.

What Can Go Wrong in a Distribution Network?

Many distribution networks achieve poor on-time, in-full delivery despite high levels of inventory. The most common problems include:

■ Poor stock availability and frequent shortages in the distribution center despite high levels of inventory and obsolescence. This is generally caused by forecast-based "push" replenishment and excessively long lead times from overseas suppliers.

■ Lack of effective processes for inventory management and replenishment of inventory in branch stores. Control of inventory and replenishment in the branch stores often rests with the branch store managers. Their main focus is usually meeting sales targets. They are typically much less focused on inventory, unless there is a shortage (which impacts sales), in which case they usually react by increasing inventory. As discussed in Chapter 5, increasing inventory in reaction to a shortage often makes things worse because it creates false demand (for the additional inventory) and may not address the root cause of the shortage. Inventory levels and the timing and quantity of replenishment are often based on "gut feel and experience" rather than any science or system.

■ Large amounts of stock are often horded in the branch stores due to the perception (often well founded) that the supply from the distribution center is unreliable. In one company I worked with, following a short-age of a range of items, one major branch raised an internal stock trans-fer for the entire national stock of every one these items. This of course ensured that they did not run out, but it was not particularly helpful for the other 59 branches needing those items.

■ Uncontrolled intracompany stock transfers. This can mean that, faced with a shortage, a branch will simply order the stock from another branch, shifting the shortage to that branch, as well as generating costs for expedited freight moving items around the country.

■ Branch stores filling shortages with locally supplied "alternative" prod-uct and even sourcing products from competitors. This often incurs a severe cost penalty and creates quality risks, as the locally sourced alternative is rarely exactly the same as the original item.

■ Local branch managers and branch sales teams identifying and sourcing new products directly from suppliers to meet particular customer needs. On the face of it, this appears to be a proactive and entrepreneurial approach. In my experience, it usually leads to disaster with a proliferation of slow-moving part numbers, quality and compliance issues caused by the lack of formal evaluation of the new products, and commercial issues due to poorly conceived sup-plier relationships.

This list reads like a bit of a horror story, but in fact, most of the industrial distribution networks I have worked with over the years have exhibited most or all these problems. Unfortunately, the problems tend to compound each other. For example, frequent shortages lead to a high level of intracompany orders and random increases in inventory to react to shortages. These in turn increase the variability of demand on the distribution center and suppliers, which makes it harder for them to meet this demand, leading in turn to more shortages. This vicious cycle ulti-mately leads to a breakdown in trust between the distribution center and the branch stores. A poisonous and costly "every man for himself" cul-ture develops. The result is then poor customer service and high levels of inventory and obsolescence.

The good news is that these problems can be overcome. Most of this book has discussed the steps you need to take to ensure that you have stock in your distribution center to ensure delivery on time and in full. However, ensuring that your branch stores have the right inventory in the right place at the right time takes some additional steps.

Designing Your Future State Distribution Network

Designing your distribution network is a balance of cost and customer service. The key cost drivers are inventory and freight. Inventory is directly related to the number of links (or "nodes") in your supply chain. As a rule of thumb, the amount of inventory you need to meet a given level of customer demand is around 40% greater if you have two warehouses (e.g., a distribution center and a branch store) than if you supplied the customer directly from one warehouse. In fact, the amount of inventory you are likely to need in a distribution network can be calculated as the inventory you calculated to meet the total demand (using the formula in Chapter 5) multiplied by the square root of the number of warehouses in which the item is stocked.* Handling and freight costs also increase the more times the goods are unloaded, received, put away, picked, staged, loaded, and shipped. Therefore, inventory and supply chain cost will generally increase as the number of links in the supply chain increases.

On the other hand, economics and suppliers often dictate that for long-haul routes, such as international shipping, you consolidate freight into large loads, such as shipping containers. Customers and branch stores usually don't have the demand to justify receiving such large quantities at once. Therefore, a distribution center is necessary for cross-docking the goods. This means unpacking the container or bulk load from the supplier and allocating the stock to separate deliveries to the various stores and customers serviced by that distribution center.

Understanding all these factors and finding the optimum supply chain structure is complex. If you have a very large distribution network, perhaps with hundreds of branch stores (such as a large retailer), there are a wide range of network design and optimization software tools available to design the optimum network. These help design the optimum freight routes and locations for distribution centers and branch stores by enabling you to model a wide range of scenarios. However, they are also costly and complex tools to set up and use. Therefore, for simpler distribution networks, we can use our favorite tool, the value stream map. Chapter 2 provides examples of how to map an extended value stream map. In Figure 11.1, we can see the current state map of the distribution network for fire extinguishers described

---

* Myerson, P. A. 2015. *Supply Chain and Logistics Management Made Easy: Methods and Application for Planning, Operations, Integration, Control and Improvement, and Network Design.* Upper Saddle River, NY: Pearson FT Press.

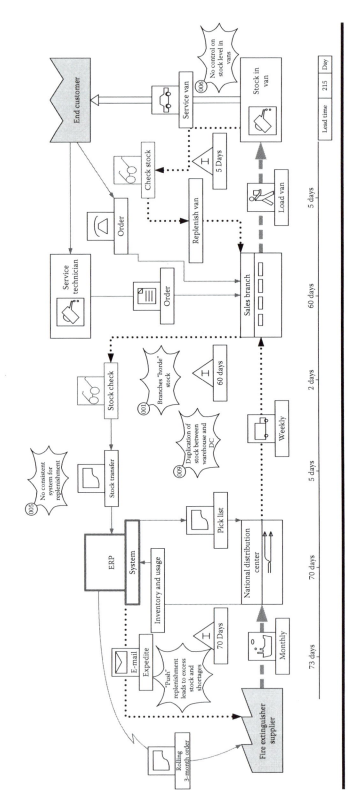

Figure 11.1   Current state value stream map of fire extinguisher distribution chain.

in Chapter 2. In this value stream a national distribution center supplied around 60 branch stores around Australia, with the 5 major branch stores in the state capitals representing the overwhelming majority of demand. These branch stores in turn replenished field service vans, which repaired and replaced extinguishers at the customers' premises. As you can see, this current state map identified many of the supply chain problems described above. Improving this takes a step-by-step approach, starting with deciding where you should have your warehouses.

Determine Where You Will Hold Your Finished Goods

The location of your customers and the length of the order lead time required by them is a key determinant in where you locate your inventory. For example, for a common item that the customer requires frequently, they may require delivery on the day of order or the next day. This will mean that the goods need to be located in a branch store close to the customer. Your customers may accept a longer order lead time on low-volume items so that they can be stocked in the distribution center rather than every branch store. Likewise, very low-volume or bespoke items may need to be ordered from your factory or suppliers as a "make-to-order" item, with a lead time equal to the total replenishment lead time.

Designing the optimum supply chain requires analysis of freight volumes and optimum freight routes and freight costs compared with the costs and inventory involved in the additional branch stores. This has to be matched to customer service expectations. A supply chain model developed in Excel or the use of one of the network optimization tools I mentioned earlier in the chapter can be useful here.

It can also be useful to calculate the total cost of fulfillment for your products. This is described in detail in *Building a Lean Fulfillment Stream* by Robert Martichenko and Kevin von Grabe.* The cost factors that need to be considered include

■ Inventory holding cost: Usually calculated as the company's weighted average cost of capital or target return on funds.

---

* Martichenko, R. and von Grabe, K. 2010. *Building a Lean Fulfillment Stream: Rethinking Your Supply Chain and Logistics to Create Maximum Value at Minimum Cost.* Cambridge, MA: Lean Enterprise Institute.

- Obsolescence and shrinkage cost: Every business will lose or have to scrap a proportion of its inventory from time to time, and the more inventory you hold, and the longer you hold it, the greater this scrap value will be.
- Warehousing cost: Usually charged per pallet or per square meter of storage space.
- Handling cost: Every time you move products in a warehouse, you add cost. For every point in your supply chain where you store goods, you have to unload, receive, put away, pick, pack, and load those goods. Each of these movements adds cost.
- Freight cost: The costs of moving goods from point to point between warehouses or from the final warehouse to the customer.

Minimizing Freight Cost

The largest single cost in a distribution network (next to the products themselves) is often freight. Many businesses waste a lot of money on freight. Typically, this waste takes the form of expedited freight of goods to fill shortages or making multiple shipments of small quantities when they could be consolidated into a single delivery.

It is important to be wary of false economies on freight. The temptation is always to look for the lowest unit cost of transport on a particular freight "leg" (the transport of goods from one point of your supply chain to the next) and end up increasing overall costs by increasing inventory or handling.

One company I worked with had its factory in a regional city and a distribution center in the capital city, around a 90-minute drive away. The business's perception was that the ability to ship full truckloads to the distribution center and backload them with raw materials coming the other way saved the company money. Certainly, the cost per pallet to transport goods from the factory to the distribution center was much lower that way. However, when total costs were analyzed, the additional handling involved with unloading goods at the distribution center and then loading them onto delivery vehicles for local delivery worked out to be more expensive than simply distributing them directly from the factory to the customer. In addition, it worked out to be cheaper to ship materials directly from the suppliers to the factory using local intercity carriers than to cross-dock and consolidate them in the distribution center.

The way you ship goods between your warehouses is largely under your own control. Recognizing this gives you an opportunity to design the optimum supply chain to reduce cost and inventory. *Fixed-interval, variable-quantity* replenishment works best in replenishing between warehouses. This means establishing a process of routine replenishment. This might be daily, weekly, or biweekly, depending on the volume of products involved, the type of freight used, and your inventory targets. As has been discussed before, the more frequently you replenish the branch stores, the lower the inventory you will need (based on our reorder point formula) and the lower the risk of shortages. If you choose a long replenishment interval, often you will find that the savings you make in regular freight will be consumed with unscheduled expedited freight to meet unexpected orders or to fill shortages. For most of the distribution networks I have worked with, branch stores are replenished at least weekly.

There is less freedom in replenishing customers. Often, the customer will dictate when they are replenished and how often. However, in many cases you can develop standard delivery routes or "milk runs." Therefore, instead of sending a separate delivery to each customer, you devise delivery routes and load your delivery vehicle with the orders for all the customers in a particular geographic region. If your network is complex, route optimization software exists, or you can develop your own system. In most networks, the key customers change infrequently, so the same delivery routes are usually set and followed each day.

Calculating the Right Level of Inventory

Once you have established your overall supply chain structure, know the demand and service expectations of your customers, decide the location of your stores, and set the frequency and timing of your replenishment, you can then calculate the amount of inventory you need. At this point, it can be very useful to build a plan for every part (PFEP) for all the products flowing through your distribution network, similar to the one we created for the inbound supply chain in Chapter 7. In this case, a PFEP will need to be created for the whole network and for each individual distribution center or branch store. Start with an overall picture for the whole network to make key decisions on where stock is held and how the network is structured.

It is also good to share an aggregated picture of customer demand that enables participants at each step of the supply chain to plan their operations to meet this demand. Ensure that upstream suppliers see this final customer demand so that they focus on meeting this rather than the "false demand" created by instability in your supply chain. Inventory levels for each point in the process are calculated using the same safety stock calculations that we introduced in Chapter 5. The demand you have to consider for each branch store is just the demand of the customers serviced from that branch store. The replenishment interval and replenishment lead time for that store are based on the ordering and delivery arrangements you have established from your distribution center or factory to that branch store.

Controlling Replenishment

We now have the network established, the freight routes determined, and the inventory levels set. The next step is to determine how the various nodes in your distribution network will be replenished.

In business, we like to encourage empowerment. As a result, it makes intuitive sense that the people running a branch store would control what stock is held in their store and the quantity and frequency of replenishment. They might even decide what items to stock in that store and who to source them from. By empowering the branch store team in this way, they will likely be more motivated to sell more. The alternative to this approach is central control, which on the face of it would seem a bureaucratic approach that removes empowerment from the people at the front line.

In my experience, the decentralized approach leads to problems. The staff in a branch store are usually salespeople who are necessarily focused on maximizing revenue and margins. They usually lack the time, expertise, and motivation to do an effective job of managing inventory or purchasing. Businesses are also usually reluctant to hold salespeople to account for inventory, because they see it as a distraction from the core sales role of selling. As a result, it is usually better that the supply chain is managed by supply chain specialists with inventory and replenishment controlled centrally.

There are some good techniques to manage this. The most common is distribution requirements planning (DRP). As the name would suggest, DRP is typically a function within an ERP system. In a DRP system, your team in the branch store have the responsibility to provide the central supply chain team with a regular sales forecast update and accurate data on the current stock on hand. The central supply chain team then sets the appropriate safety stock levels and ensures that stock is replenished to meet forecast demand. The DRP system then calculates automatically at regular intervals (usually nightly or weekly) and generates a report recommending the products that need to be sent to the branch stores. DRP calculates replenishment based on forecast, and so is subject to the vagaries of inaccurate forecasts. However, the replenishment lead time from a distribution center to a branch store is usually short. There are also generally fewer factors causing supply and demand variation, and so the flow of goods and demand are more stable. Therefore, DRP can be quite a simple and effective solution. However, while a forecast-based model can work well with DRP, a pull system will generally work even better.

Using a pull system to replenish branch stores involves essentially the same method described in Chapter 5. We recommend that the central supply chain team still calculate Kanban quantities, replenishment intervals, and stock levels, but instead of replenishing to forecast, the Kanban system will replenish based on the products sold in the previous replenishment interval. Use of Kanban cards usually proves challenging in a distribution network; therefore, many companies use the min-max functionality in their ERP to operate a reorder point pull system. For min-max to work, it is important that the branch store maintain a high level of inventory record accuracy. An alternative approach I used in one business was that every time the branch opened a new pallet of product, that triggered the reordering of a replacement pallet. The branch simply scanned the labels off the pallets they opened each week and e-mailed them to the central supply chain team.

Whether you use DRP or Kanban, the important thing is that you have a structured and consistent process for replenishing branch stores based on clear business rules. When branch store managers are able to establish their own systems based on gut feel, personal preference, or reaction to the last shortage, then the result is usually excess stock, shortages, and expediting.

Sales and Operations Planning in a Distribution Network

The nature of a distribution network is that people tend to be located all around the country. As a result, the temptation is to just involve the central supply chain team and head office functional leaders in the sales and operations planning process.

This is a mistake. As difficult as it can be, you need to involve the branch stores in the demand review step of the sales and operations planning cycle (see Chapter 4). This is because staff in the branch store are likely to be the best informed on changes in demand in their own area. Therefore, the central demand manager needs to have a regular (at least monthly) phone conference with each branch store to discuss demand and the supply chain settings, such as safety stock and the range of items held in stock.

Involving the branch stores in sales and operations planning does not contradict my previous advice to centralize supply chain control. The final decision on what to buy and what to hold needs to rest on the supply chain team. However, by allowing the branch stores input on the settings that control replenishment of their branch and gaining their insights into likely demand changes, you will get much better outcomes in terms of delivery and also better relationships between "head office" supply chain staff and the branches.

A company I worked with recently had established an excellent centralized supply chain management system for their distribution network along the lines of what I have described above. Unfortunately, the supply chain team had worked largely in isolation from the branch stores. As a result, many of the assumptions built into the supply chain model in terms of demand, product mix, and safety stock were incorrect or out of date. The branch stores were incurring frequent shortages and were deeply frustrated, as they had no way to influence the replenishment system. Many were addressing the issues by ordering stock from expensive local "alternative" suppliers or from other branches. This just shifted shortages around the country and further confused the demand picture, making things worse. The solution was for the supply chain team to communicate regularly and in a structured way with branch stores. This ensured that the central replenishment system was well understood and based on up-to-date and relevant demand data from the branches.

Importance of Good Product Management in a Distribution Network

The ease of introducing new products in a distribution business frequently leads to problems. As manufacturers, the difficulty and cost involved in introducing new products usually means that there is a rigorous approval process before product development even commences. This process can be painful if you are a salesperson, but it does ensure that there is a clear business case for the new product, that sales targets are set, and that there are clear accountabilities. In distribution businesses, these controls are often absent. Consequently, I have found many distribution businesses with large quantities of obsolete stock caused by a huge proliferation in the number of stock keeping units (SKUs).

A hardware products distributor I worked with created a large PFEP for the products distributed through their company-owned stores. What they quickly found was that they were selling a very large number of items across their network—more than 9000 SKUs, even though the largest number of SKUs held in a single store was around 2000. In many cases, different stores stocked different brands of the same item, often contradicting national agreements with key suppliers for these items. This was usually driven by branch store manager preference, and even by enterprising supplier sales representatives selling their products directly to the branch managers. Clearly, there was a lack of standardization and central control of product management, leading to excessive inventory and problems with obsolescence.

As we know from Chapter 5, the quantity of inventory you hold is directly related to the number of SKUs you stock. The quantity of inventory in terms of days cover also tends to be greater for items with lower sales volumes. Therefore, you can imagine the inventory impacts of holding 9000 SKUs when only 2000–3000 were necessary.

To avoid these problems, distribution businesses need effective processes for product management. Deciding which products to stock and in which locations must be the ultimate responsibility of the marketing function. Likewise, selecting suppliers and purchasing inventory is a purchasing and supply chain function. It is important that the staff in branch stores are allowed an input into these decisions due to their local knowledge. This input needs to be built into regular reviews of the product portfolio and, for purchasing, into the new supplier selection process. However, allowing every branch to make their own decisions on what to purchase and from whom is a recipe for supply chain disaster.

To 3PL or Not to 3PL?

The final question I constantly get asked about distribution networks is whether distribution businesses should do their own distribution at all or outsource this to a third-party logistics provider (3PL). The answer to this question is, "It depends."

Introducing a 3PL brings significant challenges. First, the 3PL provider has to make a profit; therefore, unless your warehouse and logistics are hopelessly inefficient, it is likely a 3PL arrangement will cost more. If your warehouse and logistics *are* hopelessly inefficient, I would also suggest applying some Lean thinking to make them more efficient before you go ahead and outsource.

Second, the 3PL is a separate company. You are therefore introducing an additional communication interface and often a different IT system for data to flow through before your customers get their order. This can cause confusion, errors, and delays if not set up carefully and managed well. Of course, you can get the 3PL company to use your system and even base your people on site at the 3PL, but by the time you get to this point, I find it hard to see the benefits you are getting from the 3PL arrangement compared with just renting a building and running your own warehouse. A perceived benefit of a 3PL is that you can use as much or as little warehouse space as you want. However, 3PL operators need to make a return on their warehouse investment too. It is often hard for them to find a customer to use the warehouse space you don't use and then to have it available when you need it. Therefore, most 3PL arrangements I have seen usually require the customer to take and pay for a fixed amount of space or else involve quite high per pallet storage charges for fully flexible use of space. Companies also frequently fail to deal with legacy costs associated with outsourcing, and so end up with empty warehouses and duplicated overheads (between the company and the 3PL), leading to significantly higher overall costs.

3PL arrangements do have benefits. First, if you are a manufacturer or marketing company, you might want to focus on these activities and view distribution as a "back office" function that can be outsourced. On the other hand, if you are a distributor of products under someone else's brand, then your customers might be justified in questioning what actual value you add in return for the margin you charge if all you are doing is managing the sales process.

3PL arrangements are generally more flexible than leasing or owning warehouses, as they typically involve shorter contract terms and allow you to shift, add, or remove warehouse locations based on your changing needs.

For example, a client of ours in the United Kingdom is a distributor of food ingredients to major fast-moving consumer goods companies. Using a 3PL company enables them to locate inventory next to a major customer in Ireland without the cost and risk of setting up their own Irish warehouse. Should the contract with the customer end, our customer will have a relatively simple process to exit the Irish warehouse and minimal shutdown costs.

In complex supply chains, using a 3PL can also be more effective than using separate providers at each point of the chain. For example, in the sheet metal case study in Chapter 8, we used a single 3PL provider to manage the goods from the supplier in China to our customers in Melbourne. This ensured that one company had accountability to ensure that the goods flowed on time, in full all the way through the supply chain.

While outsourcing the warehousing and handling of your products may not always make sense, it is a different story when it comes to freight. Owning and operating your own transport fleet rarely makes economic sense since road freight in particular is very competitive; there are many good carriers, and often your freight can take advantage of backloads or share space with other goods heading in the same direction. Trucks and trailers are also highly expensive assets that require costly maintenance. You are invariably better off investing your business's precious capital into assets that will grow your production and sales rather than investing it in transport equipment.

So, in summary, there is no right answer on whether you should use a 3PL. It depends on the individual needs of your business and supply chain. By value stream mapping your supply chain and calculating the end-to-end total cost of fulfillment, you will be able to objectively assess the costs and benefits of using 3PL providers for your business.

Summary

Getting products to the right customer at the right time in the right quantity and at the right price often requires a distribution network. Adding more links to your supply chain may be necessary to achieve the service levels your customers require, but will inevitably add cost and complexity. Therefore, an overriding consideration in distribution chains is to keep them as simple as possible with as few links as possible. The keys to achieving a simple and cost-effective distribution network that delivers reliable on-time, in-full delivery to customers are

- Use a value stream map to see the end-to-end flow in your distribution chain and to identify ways to eliminate lead time, cost, and waste.
- The level of customer service you need to provide will determine the structure and location of your warehouses. Don't assume that you need a branch in every town. As long as you can meet your customers' service expectations, it does not matter where the goods come from.

■ Calculate the total cost of fulfillment for your supply chain. This will enable you to make decisions about how the supply chain is set up based on total cost rather than focusing on local savings at one point or on one leg of the transport route.

■ Freight is a key cost in the supply chain, and replenishment interval is a key driver of inventory. Use milk runs and regular deliveries to enable you to deliver goods to your branch stores and customers more often without increasing freight cost.

■ Create a PFEP for your overall supply chain and for each warehouse in order to determine the right settings for inventory and replenishment.

■ Centralized control of replenishment through your distribution network is usually the most effective method. However, regular structured communication with every branch store is necessary to ensure that their input and market intelligence is incorporated into inventory and replenishment settings.

■ Disciplined product management processes are needed in distribution networks to prevent the uncontrolled proliferation of SKUs leading to high inventory, frequent shortages, and high levels of slow-moving and obsolete stock.

■ 3PLs are not a panacea for your distribution network problems. They are usually a costlier option than managing your distribution network yourself. However, their flexibility means that they have a role for many businesses where distribution is not a core function or where there is a need to frequently change supply chain structure due to changing customer needs.

Chapter 12

Bringing It All Together

What You Will Learn in This Chapter

- *An overview of how Lean supply chain thinking can address the six reasons for poor on-time, in-full delivery*
- *How to measure and improve supply chain performance*
- *Where to start on your delivery performance transformation*

Addressing the Six Reasons for Poor On-Time, In-Full Delivery

Back in Chapter 1, we identified six key reasons why businesses fail to deliver on time and in full to their customers. They were

1. The customer cannot forecast accurately.
2. Long lead times.
3. Big batch sizes and big shipment quantities.
4. Material shortages.
5. Poor factory performance.
6. Poor warehouse and logistics practices.

Through the course of this book, I have attempted to systematically address the root causes of these problems.

■ To address the problem of poor customer forecasts, you will have recognized the limitations of forecasting and avoided the use of forecast-driven material requirements planning (MRP) replenishment systems. Instead, you will have implemented pull replenishment processes that are less dependent on forecasts. You will have limited your use of forecasts to a high-level monthly overview that is a key input into your sales and operations planning system. This high-level forecast will allow you to make medium-term plans to have the resources and capacity in place to meet changes in overall demand.

■ To reduce lead times, you will have created value stream maps that enable you to understand the drivers of your lead time, including your replenishment lead time from suppliers. You will have developed a future state map that reduced lead time both within your business and within your overall supply chain.

■ To reduce batch sizes, you will have implemented a new future state map that economically reduces your batch sizes in production and allows you to order smaller amounts more frequently from your suppliers.

■ You will have addressed the three key drivers of material shortages.
  – You will have gained an understanding of the variability of your demand and used statistical safety stock to set the appropriate level of inventory for your business.
  – You will have value stream mapped your supply chain and internal procurement processes and found ways to reduce lead time.
  – You will have reduced your replenishment interval using Kanban or repetitive flexible replenishment.

■ You will have developed service level agreements with key suppliers that outline the key ground rules governing day-to-day supply. You will have also gained an understanding of your suppliers' processes and supply chains, and tailored your ordering and replenishment processes to reflect this reality. You will have also established open two-way communication with suppliers focused on constructively addressing the issues that impact supply.

■ If you are a manufacturer, your future state value stream map will have involved you identifying the pacemaker within your production process, stabilizing and leveling the flow of production downstream of that pacemaker, and using repetitive flexible supply or a product wheel to level your product mix and produce smaller quantities of your key products more frequently, giving more consistent and reliable output from production.

■ Finally, you will have improved the performance of your distribution network by setting clear rules on what gets replenished, when, and by whom; establishing routine store replenishment; and setting some clear rules around product introduction and obsolescence. Your finished goods inventory will also be set to meet demand variation and adjusted through your sales and operation planning to meet known demand changes.

In summary, you will have strategies in place to address each of the six causes of poor on-time, in-full delivery.

Measuring Supply Chain Performance

You cannot improve what you do not measure. Therefore, throughout the book I have recommended business metrics essential to driving supply chain improvement. The most important of these is delivery in full, on time (DIFOT). However, it is important to measure some of the key drivers of DIFOT. These include

■ Stock availability
■ Inventory turns or days of inventory
■ Supplier DIFOT
■ Various lead times, including order fulfillment lead time, supplier replenishment lead time, and your internal process lead time
■ Inventory record accuracy in your warehouse

As an overall metric of distribution network and supply chain performance, calculating perfect order fulfillment at each step of the extended value stream is an excellent approach. It can provide a much more detailed view of the issues through your supply chain, although putting this complex set of metrics in place may be difficult for many businesses.

Beyond these metrics, there are a wide range of other metrics you can track, and what you measure will depend on the particular problems facing your business. These include

■ *Performance to plan*: This can simply be the number of scheduled orders completed each week compared with the total number of orders scheduled for completion that week. This provides a measure of whether manufacturing is on track, as well as a measure of whether the production plan is realistic.

■ *Forecast accuracy*: The supply chain management gurus would say this is the most important metric. I see it as fairly unimportant, since I do not recommend using a forecast to drive day-to-day and week-to-week replenishment. However, a high-level forecast accuracy measure can be useful for fine-tuning your sales and operations planning process. A simple forecast accuracy can be the ratio of total monthly throughput on each value stream or production line to the forecast for that month. I would suggest you measure this for a time horizon consistent with your overall material replenishment lead time. Therefore, forecast accuracy one month out is probably less important than the accuracy of the forecast three to six months out.

■ *Bill of materials and routing accuracy*: This is a measure of the health of your master data in your enterprise resource planning (ERP) system and is the ratio of the number of bills of materials and routings that are complete and accurate to the total number of bills and routings reviewed.

■ *Number of back orders*: Some businesses do not have back orders, while others have dozens or even hundreds of them. Items on back order are an indicator of a DIFOT failure, as well as a predictor of future DIFOT failure since items on back order are by definition out of stock and cannot be supplied. Therefore, maintaining a simple count of back orders and trying to drive this to zero will drive improved DIFOT.

■ *Picking errors*: Another factor that can impact DIFOT is picking accuracy. Clearly, if warehouse operators are picking the wrong items or the wrong quantities, this will impact your DIFOT. Simply count the number of errors found at final checking and manifesting of orders, and for a further measure, track the number of credits or customer complaints due to incomplete or incorrect deliveries.

Improving Your Supply Chain Metrics

There is not much point in measuring things if you are not going to improve them. As you will have learned through this book, the secret to an effective supply chain is to design it from the ground up to deliver excellent customer service. However, even the best-designed supply chain will have problems, and it is important that these problems are used as opportunities to learn and improve. There are some key points to driving supply chain improvement effectively through your business:

- *Measure as frequently as you can.* You should record your key supply chain metrics, including DIFOT, every day, if possible. This means that you can respond to problems the next day, minimizing the impact on customers and your business. Other metrics should be measured at the shortest interval that makes sense. I would recommend measuring stock-outs and back orders (if you have them) daily, and perhaps lead time weekly and supplier DIFOT monthly.
- *Discuss supply chain performance regularly and in a structured way.* If you are measuring metrics every day, then you should be discussing and improving them every day. A daily stand-up meeting with the key supply chain team members (i.e., warehousing, operations, customer service, and planning) should occur at a set time every day and follow a set agenda. This agenda should include the previous day's performance, targets for the current day, obstacles that may prevent achievement of today's targets, and countermeasures to overcome those obstacles and ensure the target is achieved. A good structured daily stand-up meeting should take no longer than 10 minutes.
- *Every supply chain failure is an opportunity to learn.* When we start measuring something, it usually improves. This is commonly called the "halo effect," where the focus on the metric will often drive a quick improvement. This improvement will not be sustained unless the underlying causes of poor performance are addressed. Therefore, for each supply chain failure, there needs to be a corrective action. By measuring DIFOT every day, you will hopefully be only dealing with a few failures and shortages each day. The aim is to discuss each one, identify the root causes using the "five whys" or another simple analysis tool, agree on corrective actions, and then track that these corrective actions

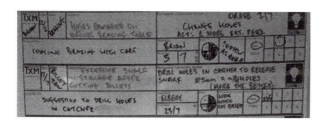

Figure 12.1   Example of concern strips used to solve simple everyday problems.

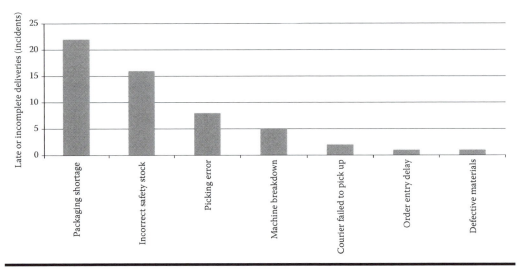

Figure 12.2   Pareto chart showing typical range of causes for delivery failure.

prevent reoccurrence of the problem. Magnetic "concern strips," shown in Figure 12.1, are a good tool to do this.

■ *Systemic problems need deeper analysis.* Simple day-to-day problems can be solved using concern strips, but complex problems may need use of more advanced root cause analysis tools, such as fishbone diagrams and A3 problem-solving worksheets. Build a Pareto chart ranking the causes of delivery failures, such as the one shown in Figure 12.2. Focus then on addressing the root cause of the largest number of late deliveries.

The Wrong Measures Drive the Wrong Behavior

Hopefully by now it is clear that the collective role of the people involved in your supply chain is to deliver the highest level of on-time, in-full delivery to your customers. Obviously, for you to stay in business, this performance needs to be achieved at the lowest level of inventory and total cost. The way you measure individuals within your team can have a profound effect on this.

For example, many businesses measure purchasing teams on the value of savings they deliver. Inevitably, these measures focus solely on the unit costs of the goods purchased. This will often lead to businesses choosing the cheapest supplier regardless of lead times, quality, and delivery performance. Much of the huge outsourcing wave of the last decade has been driven by simple unit cost savings, and has left companies with large problems with excessive inventory, poor stock availability, expediting, and inevitably, higher overall costs.

In operations as well, the wrong measures can drive the wrong behaviors. For example, many businesses focus heavily on machine performance measures such as downtime or overall equipment effectiveness (OEE). The consequence of this is that operations managers are driven to run large batch sizes and inflexible schedules in order to maximize throughput and OEE. This can often undermine efforts to improve service to customers.

Another mistake businesses make is to set overall targets for inventory reduction without understanding the drivers of inventory. One company we worked with had an arbitrary 30% inventory reduction target applied by their corporate head office. The ambitious supply chain manager, keen to impress head office, simply responded by stopping or reducing ordering. The result was widespread shortages, expediting, and in fact, overall inventory increased as the factory filled up with incomplete work in progress waiting for parts to arrive.

Bringing It All Together: The Industrial Chemicals Case Study

When Greg Boek, one of the Lean specialists at my consulting company, started working with the industrial chemicals company that I introduced in Chapter 1, he quickly found that they were experiencing every single one of the six reasons for poor delivery. This was leading to very poor on-time, in-full delivery, excessive inventory, and high costs for expedited transport. It is a scenario that we have seen over and over again. However, as you will understand from the past 11 chapters, there is a straightforward and practical pathway to supply chain improvement through application of Lean thinking.

At the heart of the solution lies the value stream map. Greg coached a small team from the chemicals company to map the end-to-end supply chain from their raw material suppliers through to the distribution networks. This highlighted many of the problems outlined above, including excessive inventory of the wrong things, long lead times, big batches, and overreliance on largely meaningless forecasts.

The solution started with reducing lead times by shortening production cycles and reducing batch sizes, as described in Chapter 6. Finished goods inventory levels were reset, and a Kanban system was put in place to trigger replenishment from the factory, as described in Chapter 5. Combining this with smaller batch sizes and shorter replenishment lead times, inventory could be reduced at the same time as reducing the number of stock-outs.

At the same time, inventory and replenishment of materials needed to be improved. A plan for every part was established, as described in Chapter 7, and Kanban replenishment put in place for raw materials and packaging.

Leveling and stabilizing the flow of production led to more consistent factory output, and the shorter lead times and replenishment cycles enabled the factory to respond more quickly to problems or changes in demand.

The result is that on-time, in-full delivery has improved from less than 80% to more than 95%. This improvement has curtailed the loss of business and enabled the sales team to start selling again with confidence that commitments to new customers will be met. As a result, the business has started to grow again.

Getting Started on Transforming Your Delivery Performance

Often, when we go to make change in our business, it is the first step that is the hardest. Unfortunately, too many businesses think that the solution to every supply chain challenge starts with new software. The reality is that the solutions to *all* business problems start with people. Supply chain is no exception.

It is important that the key managers responsible in your business first recognize that the current performance is a problem and that a significant change in business processes will be necessary to achieve this improvement.

Second, business leadership must believe that performance *can* be improved. Too often, I hear managers give me reasons why their poor supply chain performance is out of their control—supplier lead times are too long, customer demand too volatile, and the process too unreliable to achieve improved delivery. As you will have gathered by now, I believe that the solutions to these problems *are* in your business control, and you must believe that you can improve them if you are to achieve your delivery goals.

If you find in this process that your existing team are unable or (worse) unwilling to support the kind of changes likely to improve delivery performance, then you will need to address this before going further. Usually, this might involve bringing in a supply chain or operational manager with the right expertise. The aim is to get a critical mass for change, rather than trying to change everyone. Complete restructuring is likely to take too long, cost too much, and involve too much risk. It is likely as the change proceeds that individuals who are initially resistant will either change their view or decide to move into another role where their skills are better suited. It is only when individuals are actively disrupting or sabotaging the change process that should you consider more drastic action.

Once you have your team in place, the next step is to set some realistic goals. Start with your business strategy. What is it that your business is trying to achieve? Who are the priority markets and customers, and what do they expect in terms of service? Very few businesses achieve perfect delivery of every product all the time; therefore, you have to decide what is the level of service that your customers will want and accept? It is important that your improvement effort is focused first on the customers and markets that are the priority for your businesses, and if compromises have to be made, that they do not come at the expense of key customers.

The next step for many businesses is to actually start measuring performance. This should start with establishing an *honest* and simple DIFOT measure and reporting it every day if possible. You can then introduce the other key measures, such as inventory turns (or days cover), stock-outs, and lead times. When you start measuring these things, you may initially be shocked by your poor level of performance. Treat this as a positive opportunity for your business. It is much easier to improve something that is bad than to make incremental improvements to something that is already good.

Your demand history is the other key piece of data that you will need. This is usually your daily or weekly sales history by product in units for the previous 12 months. This important data is going to enable you to understand the patterns in your customer demand, such as seasonality and trends. It is the basis for building your high-level forecast and for determining the optimum level of inventory. It will also help you understand your product mix, enable you to calculate takt time, and determine your key production scheduling parameters.

Once you have your team in place, your goals clear, and some baseline data, then you are ready to start developing your first current state value stream map. Your supply chain improvement journey starts from there. So head back to Chapter 2 and away you go!

The Right Supply Chain Manager

Throughout this book, I have talked about the important role of the supply chain manager. In very small businesses, this might be combined with a production or warehouse manager role, but in most medium to large businesses, supply chain management will be a separate function. In some cases, the supply chain manager might report to operations or, alternatively, the operation manager report to the supply chain manager. Both can work, but in most cases, the supply chain manager will report directly to the general manager. So what makes a good supply chain manager?

In my view, the supply chain role oversees the whole flow of products from your suppliers, through your business, to your customer. The supply chain manager therefore needs to have the ability to understand the whole supply chain and how it connects together. Individuals who have a narrow focus, such as warehouse or buying, often (but not always) struggle to take this overview. The supply chain manager may have a role in commercial negotiations, but it is not his or her primary role. It is better to have a supply chain manager focused on the overall fulfillment process and to employ others (perhaps reporting to the supply chain manager) to focus on negotiating the deals.

Supply chain managers come from diverse academic backgrounds. Relatively few will have formal supply chain management qualifications, but a tertiary qualification in science, mathematics, business, or engineering combined with relevant supply chain experience is necessary. Interestingly, some of the best supply chain managers I have worked with have had a finance and accounting background; however, I think their success had more to do with their highly developed numerical and analytical skills than their focus on finances. Even if the supply chain manager is not actually transacting in your ERP systems and other systems, he or she needs to have a deep understanding of how they work. He or she also needs to be able to extract and analyze the data needed using tools such as spreadsheets.

While it is important that he or she understand the numbers, the supply chain manager is a key leader in your business. He or she needs to be able to develop an effective team and articulate a vision to that team. The supply chain manager will also need to develop productive relationships with external stakeholders, such as suppliers, freight and logistics providers, and sometimes customers. Finally, he or she will need to be able to effectively influence his or her peers every month in the sales and operations planning process. Therefore, good leadership, influencing, and communication skills are essential, in addition to high-level numerical reasoning skills and confidence with information technology (IT).

It sounds like a tall order, but an individual with the right personal attributes will quickly gain an understanding of how your supply chain works. In reality, the math is pretty simple—there is just a lot of it.

Do You Need a Consultant?

I lead a successful Lean consultancy, and we do a lot of supply chain work, so you could perhaps expect a self-serving answer here. However, I feel that improving on-time, in-full delivery is a core function of your supply chain manager and his or her team. It is what they are employed to do. Therefore, I would be concerned if they outsourced the whole task of improvement to an external expert. In many businesses, there is a role for consultants. There is a lot of merit in getting external expertise to facilitate the value stream mapping process. An experienced external facilitator will be able to come in with an open mind, and bring in experiences and ideas from other businesses that will add value to the knowledge existing in your business. Also, the supply chain involves a number of business functions that often have different perspectives on the problem and different ideas on the likely solution. An external expert can help bring your team together across organizational silos to agree on a future state that everyone can support.

In addition, to value stream facilitation skills, an external expert may bring in expertise that your business lacks. There are good books on how to implement many of the tools, but the prospect of building your first plan for every part, setting up your first Kanban system, or establishing your first one-piece flow cell is a lot less daunting when you have the assistance of someone who has done it many times before.

A Final Word

While many of the solutions to your supply chain problems involve relatively simple techniques, the discipline and commitment taken to implement and sustain these techniques are not easy. Improving delivery will require a significant investment in time and resources. It will also involve compromises. Not every customer can be served perfectly. Inventory may need to go up before it can go down. The cheapest supplier in terms of unit cost may not be the cheapest when all the costs of supply are considered. Likewise, the cheapest option on freight might lock you in on long lead times and large shipments, which drive high inventory and poor delivery. There will be clever work-arounds that enable you to "have your cake and eat it to," but inevitably there will need to be trade-offs between inventory and delivery, on the one hand, and cost, on the other. However, to have a successful, sustainable, and growing business, you *must* be able to deliver your customers what they need when they need it and meet their overall service expectation. To fail to do so is to fail the most basic requirement of any manufacturing or distribution business. As you have hopefully seen through the course of this book, failing your customers on delivery is so *unnecessary*. Good luck!

Index

B

Back flushing, 140
Back orders, 172
Back-to-back order, *see* Make-to-order
    finished goods strategy
Big batches, 4–5
Bill of materials, and routing accuracy, 172
Boek, Greg, 175
Bottleneck process, 46–49
Breaking through to Flow, 87–88
Building a Lean Fulfillment Stream, 159
Bullwhip effect, 5, 143, 144

C

Capacity model, 43–46
Chief financial officer (CFO), 2
CNC, *see* Computer numerically controlled
    (CNC) machining
Color-coded Kanban squares, 70
Computer numerically controlled (CNC)
    machining, 79
Currency volatility, and relative inflation, 122
Customer order lead time, 15
Custom sheet metal components, 124–126
Cycle counts, 72
Cycle time, and takt time, 43–45

D

Delivery in full, on time (DIFOT), 13–15,
    171, 172

Demand, and supply variability, 106–107
Demand management, 31, 38–39
Demand review, 50, 51–52
DIFOT, *see* Delivery in full, on time
    (DIFOT)
Distribution network, 153
    calculating level of inventory, 161–162
    common problems, 155–156
    controlling replenishment, 162–163
    cost factors, 159–160
    designing future state, 157–158
    importance of good product
        management in, 164–165
    key elements of, 154–155
    minimizing freight cost, 160–161
    need, 154
    sales and operations planning in,
        163–164
    third-party logistics provider (3PL),
        165–167
Distribution requirements planning (DRP),
    162–163
Dock-to-dock value stream, 25
Downstream distribution, 153
DRP, *see* Distribution requirements planning
    (DRP)
Dual sourcing, 137–138

E

Enterprise resource planning (ERP)
    system, 6, 13, 30, 35, 67, 78,
    139–152

accurate master data, 149
go-live dates, 151
implementing, 147–148
multilevel bills of materials, 149–151
overview, 140–141
problem with, 141–145
purchase, 145
selecting, 145–147
training and support, 151
Ex-stock finished goods strategy, 58
Extended value stream map, 25

F

Factory performance, 7–8
Finished goods strategy, 58
First-in, first-out (FIFO), 18–19
Fixed-quantity variable-interval
        replenishment, 66
Forecasting, 29–40
    accuracy, 172
    building, 32–34
    demand management, 38–39
    future, 30–31
    generating, 36–37
    importance of significance, 32
    low-volume products and
        materials, 36
    problem, 3–4
    promise of, 29–30
    raw material requirements, 34–36
    sensitivity analysis, 37–38
    tools, 38
    and weather, 31–32
Forrester effect, *see* Bullwhip effect
Freight cost, 101, 160–161

G

Glenday, Ian, 87, 90, 91, 119
Glenday sieve, 87, 113

H

Halo effect, 173
Handling cost, 160
Hub and spoke model, 154

I

Inbound supply chain, 95–108
    demand and supply variability, 106–107
    material inventory, 98–100
    material shortages, 97–98
    replenishment interval, 100–102
    risk factors for raw material shortages, 100
    supplier lead time, 103–106
Industrial chemicals case study, 175–176
Information flow, 19, 20
Information processing lead time, 16
International supply chain, 109–123
    case study, 124–126
    imported materials and risk of shortages,
        121–123
    monthly demand, 119–120
    reducing lead time in, 111
    shipment frequency and variability,
        111–119
    very low-volume materials, 120
Intracompany stock transfers, 156
Inventory, 157
    calculating safety stock, 61–64
    factors affecting, 60–61
    holding, 57–58, 121, 159
    Kanban cards, 67–70
    knee-jerk reflexive response, 64–65
    make-to-order finished goods strategy,
        58–59
    managing finished goods strategy, 59
    managing make-to-order supply, 72–74
    pull system, 70
    record accuracy, 72
    stock-outs, 71–72
    types of pull replenishment, 65–67
    virtual Kanban, 71

J

Jones, Dan, 25
Just-in-time concept, 18

K

Kanban cards, 67–70, 102, 163
Knee-jerk reflexive response, 64–65

L

Large shipments, 4–5
Lead time, 4, 15–17
Lean
   approach, 17–19
   consultancy, 179
   supply chain, 66
Lean RFS, 88
Learning to See, 23
Load leveling box, 82–84

M

Machine-driven processes, 45
Make-to-order finished goods strategy,
   58–59
Make-to-order items, 59
Make-to-order supply, 72–74
Make-to-stock finished goods strategy, 58
Make-to-stock items, 59
Making Materials Flow, 98
Martichenko, Robert, 159
Master production schedule (MPS),
   141, 142
Material inventory, 98–100
Material requirements planning (MRP), 18,
   78–79, 141–142, 144–145
Material shortages, 6, 97–98
Minimum stock, 60, 102
MPS, *see* Master production schedule (MPS)
MRP, *see* Material requirements planning
   (MRP)
Multilevel bills of materials, 149–151

N

Non-value-added activity, 21

O

Obsolescence, and shrinkage cost, 160
Obsolescence, management of, 122
OEE, *see* Overall equipment effectiveness
   (OEE)
OEMs, *see* Original equipment
   manufacturers (OEMs)

One-piece flow, 18
On time, and in full delivery, 169–171
On-time delivery, 41–43
Order fulfillment lead time, 15–16
Original equipment
   manufacturers (OEMs), 137
Overall equipment effectiveness
   (OEE), 175
Overseas suppliers, 121–122

P

Pacemaker process, 81–82, 86–87, 93
Pacemakers, and pitch, 86–87
Pareto chart, 174
PFEP, *see* Plan for every part (PFEP)
Picking errors, 172
Pitch interval, 82, 84–86, 93
Plan–do–check–act problem-solving
   method, 64
Plan for every part (PFEP), 98–99,
   112–113, 161
Powder coating, 82
Process flow, 19, 20
Product family, 20
Production scheduling, 77–94
   choosing pitch interval, 84–86
   leveling product mix, 91
   managing flow with pacemaker, 81–82
   manufacturing sequence, 87
   measure and pitch interval, 82
   overview of pacemakers and pitch,
     86–87
   planning question, 78–79
   planning scenario, 79–81
   product mix and product cycle, 87–90
   product wheels, 91–92
   repetitive flexible supply (RFS), 90–91
   using load leveling box, 82–84
Product life cycles, 122
Product mix
   leveling, 91
   and product cycle, 87–90
Product wheels, 91–92
Pull replenishment, 65–67
Pull system, 17–19, 70
Push production, 17–19, 81

Q

Quality problem, 121

R

Raw material shortages, 100
Reorder point, *see* Minimum stock
Repetitive flexible supply (RFS), 90–91, 112
Replenishment interval, 100–102, 116
Replenishment lead time, 16, 60
RFS, *see* Repetitive flexible supply (RFS)
Roadrunner production, 8
Rother, Mike, 23

S

Safety stock, 61–64
Sales, and operations planning (S&OP), 41–56
    advanced capacity models, 46–49
    capacity at bottleneck process, 46–49
    cycle time and takt time, 43–45
    demand review, 51–52
    in distribution network, 163–164
    matching capacity to demand, 41–43
    meeting, 53–54
    overview of, 55
    process, 49–51
    supply review, 52–53
Sales conference, 1–2
Salespeople, 2
S&OP, *see* Sales, and operations planning
        (S&OP)
Seeing the Whole, 25
Service level agreement, 132
Shipment frequency, and variability, 111–119
Shook, John, 23
Signal card, 19
SKU, *see* Stock keeping unit (SKU)
Standard deviation, 62, 64
Stock keeping unit (SKU), 38, 165
Stock-outs, 71–72
Suppliers, 127–138
    basic rules for working with, 130–131
    establishing service level agreement, 132
    good, 127–128
    importance of metrics, 134–136

internal processes, 132–133
    lack of communication, 131–132
    lead time, 103–106
    poor performance, 136–138
    purchase order, 133–134
    understanding, 128–129
Supply chain, 43, 11–27, 157, 159
    definition, 12–13
    delivery in full, on time (DIFOT), 13–15
    delivery performance, 176–177
    improving metrics, 172–174
    lead time, 15–17
    and Lean approach, 17–19
    manager, 177–178
    measuring, performance, 171–172
    takt time, 17
    with value stream map, 19–25
Supply review, 50–51, 52–53

T

Takt time, 17, 43–45
Third-party logistics provider (3PL),
        165–167
3PL, *see* Third-party logistics provider (3PL)
Time interval, 33
Two-bin system, 68

V

Value-added activity, 21
Value stream map, 19–25, 103
Variable-quantity fixed-interval
        replenishment, 66
Virtual Kanban system, 71, 102
von Grabe, Kevin, 159

W

Warehouse, and logistics practices, 8
Warehousing cost, 121, 160
Waste, 19
Womack, Jim, 25

Z

Z score, 62–63